ANATOMY OF HUMANS

ANATOMY
OF
HUMANS

INCLUDING WORKS BY LEONARDO DA VINCI,
JOHN FLAXMAN, HENRY GRAY AND OTHERS

IAN SIMPSON

CRESCENT BOOKS
NEW YORK

ACKNOWLEDGEMENT

To Melissa Denny, for her editorial and research work on this book

PHOTO CREDITS

PLATES 2–39, 41–44; 111–117, BRITISH MUSEUM, LONDON; FIG. IV, PLATES 45–89, BERNARD QUARITCH, LONDON; PLATES 40 AND 41, ROYAL COLLEGE OF SURGEONS, LONDON; PLATE 1, VICTORIA AND ALBERT MUSEUM, LONDON; FIGS. II AND III, WINDSOR CASTLE, ROYAL LIBRARY, © 1990 HER MAJESTY THE QUEEN; FIG. V, ROYAL COLLEGE OF PHYSICIANS, EDINBURGH; FIG. I, MARY EVANS PICTURE LIBRARY, LONDON.

This 1991 edition published by Crescent Books, distributed by Outlet Book Company, Inc., a Random House Company, 225 Park Avenue South, New York, New York 10003

ISBN 0-517-05394-2
87654321

Printed and bound in Hong Kong

CONTENTS

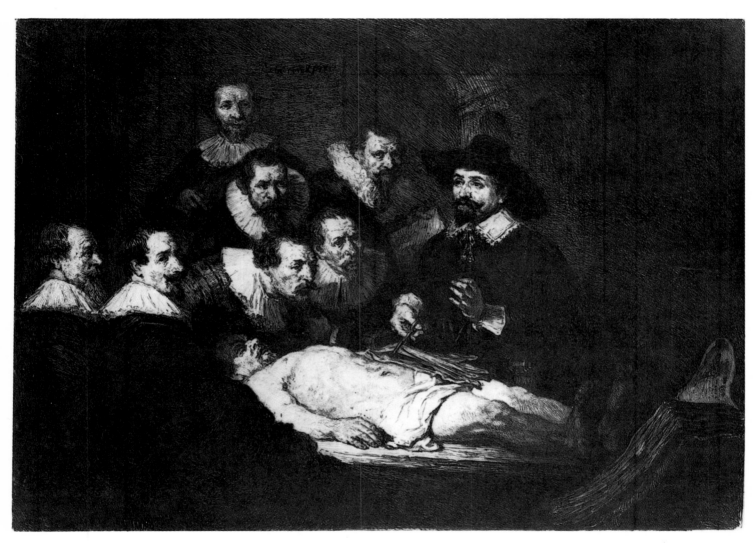

Fig i
REMBRANDT VAN RIJN, *The Anatomy Lesson*, 1632, etching.
This etching was made after Rembrandt's famous group portrait of the Amsterdam Guild of
Surgeons attending an anatomy lesson given by Dr Tulp. Photograph: Mary Evans Picture
Library.

INTRODUCTION

No matter when an anatomical book was published, its illustrations always hold a particular fascination: they have the power to communicate information to the non-specialist, transcending language barriers and expressing in simple, graphic form ideas which many pages of text may not be able adequately to explain. Moreover, illustrations give us a fascinating insight into the attitudes of the time, revealing how artistic techniques have changed and styles of visual communication developed.

Perhaps what fascinates us most about anatomical illustrations is the fact that they contribute to our awareness of ourselves. They help us to understand more completely how we are constructed, and how we function. Our present understanding of the 'human machine' is based on the way in which it has been understood in the past.

This book focuses on published anatomical illustration in the eighteenth and nineteenth centuries, a period of enormous social and artistic change as well as of scientific discovery. Included also are several examples of the finest early work, by artists such as Leonardo da Vinci, Eustachio and Vesalius, whose anatomical studies provide a fascinating contrast to later attitudes and styles.

Some of the earliest medical manuscripts are herbals — hand-illustrated books identifying medicinal plants; these were intended to be entirely practical, though are now regarded as works of art. Anatomical subjects, mostly depicting operations of various sorts, also appear in manuscripts, as do naïve figures with the main muscles, arteries and veins highlighted. These drawings were known only to a limited circle of people, since they could only be disseminated by copying. Eventually woodcuts were used to enable illustrations to be printed, and after the introduction of the printing press in the fifteenth century, wider circulation meant that medical knowledge was made more generally available. The often delightful illustrations in these early works show how haphazard was the knowledge of human anatomy in the fifteenth and early sixteenth centuries. Before the Reformation the dissection of human corpses had been prohibited by the Catholic Church; it had therefore to be done illegally and ignorance was widespread.

The first detailed anatomical studies began in the Renaissance, the period which produced so many great artists and also marked the beginning of an explosion of interest in things scientific. However, it was not only through medical science that the true study of anatomy began, but through the study of the human body by artists. They observed human proportions, investigated the muscular structure and the way in which the body moved, and this first external examination of 'surface anatomy', as it were, was quickly extended further to include the underlying muscles, blood vessels and nervous system.

One of the artists who was most interested in anatomy as a science was Leonardo da Vinci (1452–1519). His interest in aeronautics and engineering is well known, but he also turned his formidable mind to human anatomy. Although Leonardo's first anatomical studies date from 1490, it was in 1500, after a period spent in Milan, that he became engrossed in the study of man's anatomy from birth to death. In the early years of the sixteenth century he dissected more than thirty corpses and his conclusions, written in his famous left-handed mirror writing, prefigured many later studies.

Leonardo found that existing texts were at variance with what he could deduce from dissection and he decided to produce his own textbook, writing 'This work is to begin with the conception of man'. In his notebooks he outlines the systematic illustration of the skeleton and various parts of the body to demonstrate myology, angiology and neurology, and includes studies of muscles and the proportions of the body. He also planned to include a separate study of the female figure. In a note written in 1510 Leonardo said that the complete understanding of the human body could not be achieved by words alone: 'the more thoroughly you describe, the more you will confuse . . .. It is therefore necessary to draw as well as to describe'. Apart from the skill and virtuosity that he brought to his anatomical drawings, he also devised new ways in which to present them with a powerful realistic effect. In his drawings of the skeleton, for example, he shaded the background, so that the bone structure is thrown into sharp relief, a 'trick' taken up by Albinus in his *Tabulae Sceleti* (1747) (see plates 26–30). Leonardo also brought to anatomical drawing the idea of illustrating the different layers and systems of the body in logical succession. He considered that for this purpose eight drawings were required, starting with the individual bones, then the skeleton with ligaments, next the muscles and continuing through the layers of tendons to the nerves, veins, arteries and, finally, the skin. Interestingly, he used cross-sections, perhaps an idea adapted from architectural drawing, to show the relationship between the various layers.

Though Leonardo's book on anatomy was never published, his drawings would have been available for study by contemporary scientists, and remained accessible after his death in 1519 until 1570. He did therefore have a great influence on the perception and depiction of human anatomy.

Anatomical illustration, as soon as it became based on direct observation, presented a dilemma that was never really resolved. This is the question as to whether the artist should depict a particular body, with all its individual oddities, or whether the drawing should represent the synthesis of knowledge based on evidence derived from several sources. This dichotomy is best seen in comparing plates 1 and 2, Eustachio's figure being a formalised

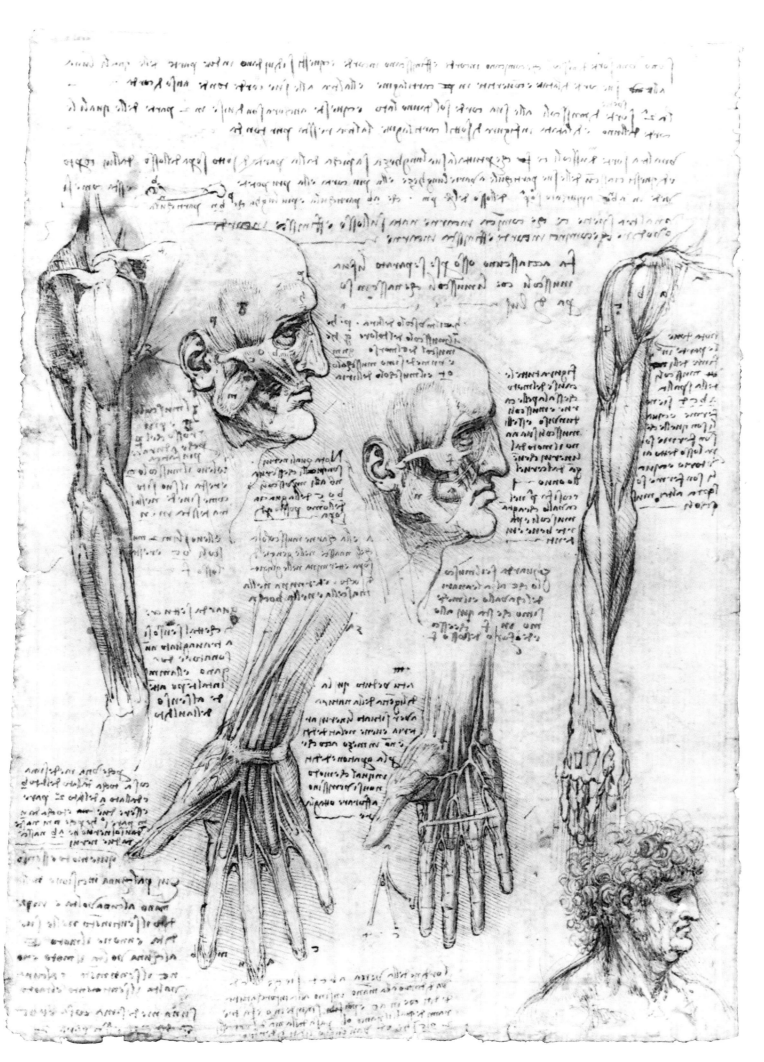

Fig ii

LEONARDO DA VINCI, anatomical drawing of the muscles of the arm, shoulder, hand and
face, c.1510, pen and ink. Photograph: Windsor Castle, Royal Library.

mannequin, whereas Vesalius' bodies are far more dramatically 'real', supported by ropes and with their flayed skin hanging off them.

Vesalius' *De Humani Corporis Fabrica* represents the first great milestone in anatomical illustration. A work of 663 pages, it was published when Vesalius was only 28 and a lecturer in surgery at the University of Padua. It had more than 200 woodcut illustrations, including a title page showing him giving an anatomy lesson. The book was intended to publicise Vesalius' lectures and to be a teaching aid for a wider audience. The illustrations were to be an adequate 'substitute' for a human body, if that were not available. The book provided a text from which those who had attended his lectures could demonstrate his theories to others and he claimed that 'every small part of the human body' was represented in detail, and that in addition instructions were given for the correct dissection and surgical techniques.

No text book like this had been attempted before, though Eustachio was intending to produce a similarly innovative work, with copperplate illustrations, which was never published. The importance that was attached to Vesalius' work, however, is indicated by the fact that scientists continued to search for lost plates until they were found and published in Rome in 1714, almost 200 years after they were made.

Vesalius' illustrator was possibly a Flemish artist, but little is known about him. The illustrations were much copied and an anatomical compendium by Thomas Germinus printed in London in 1545 included several such copies in the form of copperplate engravings. These are among the earliest English metal engravings and the book is closely connected with Henry VIII's efforts to raise the standard of surgery in England.

Germinus' book was itself copied in Germany, where they were also striving to improve professional standards and where dissection and surgery courses were much needed. These courses required a manual for the students and often also for the instructor; Vesalius provided this with another work, *Epitome*. Like *De Humani Corporis Fabrica*, it explained anatomy with illustrations in the absence of a dissected body, and by the second half of the sixteenth century such textbooks were much in demand.

Anatomical demonstrations continued into the seventeenth century and appear in many instances to have become something of a public performance. Rembrandt (1600–1669), established his early reputation with a painting entitled *The Anatomy Lesson of Dr Tulp*, dated 1632 (see fig. i). This was a commissioned group portrait of the Amsterdam Guild of Surgeons watching a demonstration by Dr Tulp and it shows the importance attached to the study of anatomy at that time.

Over a hundred years later Johann Zoffany (1733–1810) painted the *Anatomy Lesson at the Academy* which shows the distinguished surgeon William Hunter (1718–83) lecturing at the Royal Academy (see fig. v). Hunter, who was Professor of Anatomy at the Academy, is not carrying out

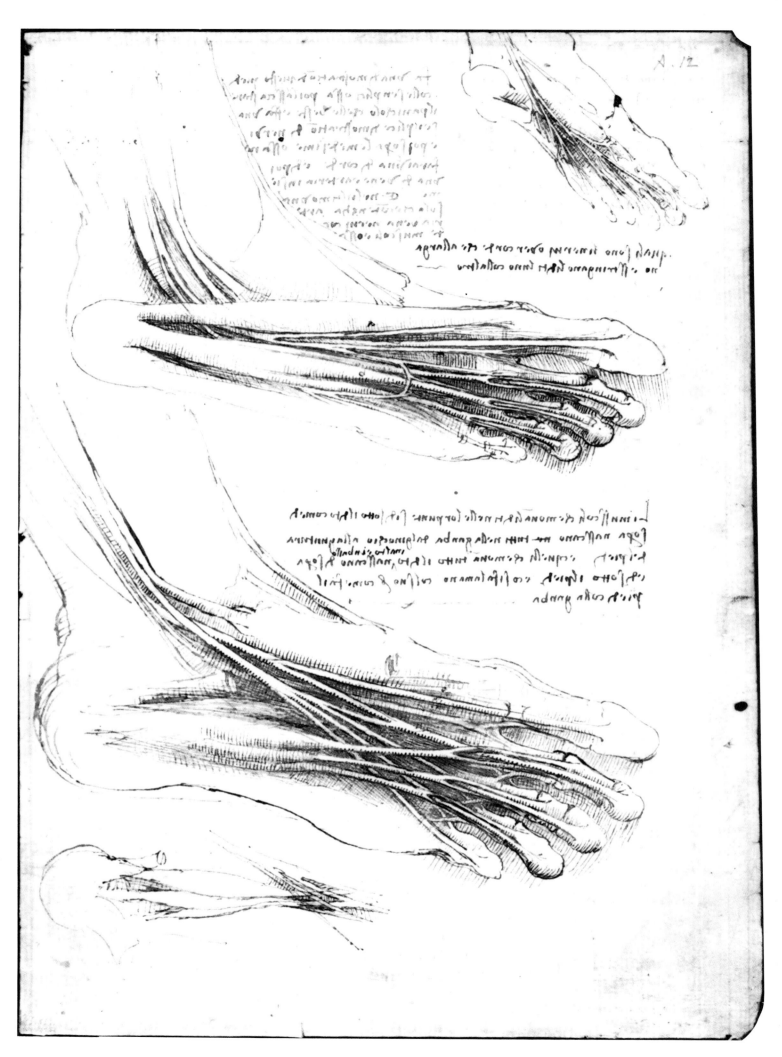

Fig iii
LEONARDO DA VINCI, anatomical drawing of the foot, c.1510, pen and ink. Photograph:
Windsor Castle, Royal Library.

a dissection but has a live male model, a cast of a naked man and a skeleton as visual aids for his lecture. Painted around 1775, it is not certain who many of the members of his audience are, although one of them is identifiable as Joshua Reynolds, President of the Royal Academy.

William Hunter, the lecturer in Zoffany's painting, was himself the author of a famous anatomical book, the *Gravid Uterus*. To illustrate this book Hunter employed a Dutch artist who had come to live in England, Jan Van Rymsdyk. By 1750 Rymsdyk was in London making anatomical drawings for Hunter; he may have had earlier experience of anatomical drawing because his earliest drawings for Hunter are very accomplished. Rymsdyk has been called the 'father' of British medical illustration, but apart from his drawings for William Hunter and other eminent physicians of the time, there is little known about him.

William Hunter's *Gravid Uterus* took more than twenty years to reach publication and Rymsdyk worked intermittently on illustrations for the book over this period of time. After this long period of contact between author and illustrator it is all the more surprising that in his preface to the book Hunter makes no reference to Rymsdyk, though the engraver of two of the plates received lavish praise. This lack of recognition of Rymsdyk's contribution was not because Hunter did not appreciate his work. He carefully preserved the original drawings he commissioned from Rymsdyk and on the death of William Smellie, another physcian who had commissioned work from the artist, he bought Rymsdyk's drawings from the estate. Many of the greatest anatomical illustrations of the second half of the eighteenth century were by Rymsdyk, who worked not only for William Hunter and William Smellie but for other eminent figures in the medical world like Charles Jenty and John Hunter, William Hunter's brother.

However, Rymsdyk's ambition was to be a society portrait painter; perhaps he thought that his contact with the medical profession would gain him introduction to likely sitters. From time to time he abandoned medical illustration: he spent 1758–59 in Bristol, then second only to London as a prosperous commercial centre, painting portraits of eminent Bristol citizens, and visiting again in 1762 and 1764.

The illustrations made from Rymsdyk's drawings are remarkable not for any highly personal drawing style, but because of his objective and craftsmanlike approach to illustration. His highly detailed drawings look remarkably photographic but he was careful to select those details which would communicate clearly what he could see and their detached, objective quality belies the fact that they often had to be produced at great speed from dissection subjects that were rapidly decaying.

Rymsdyk's drawings, reproduced in the form of mezzotint and copper engravings, were used extensively in medical teaching, and individual plates were framed and displayed in lecture theatres and dissecting rooms. These illustrations played a very important part in medical education both

Fig iv

PETER PAUL RUBENS, studies of arms, undated, pen and ink. Photograph: Bernard
Quaritch. Rubens, one of the seventeenth century artists most celebrated for his sensuous
treatment of the human body, is here exploring the musculature of the half-bent arm. Drawn
very freely, the pen emphasizes the rather serpentine, and occasionally distorted,
forms which characterize his paintings.

in Britain and in the United States where Rymsdyk's drawings which were made for Charles Jenty are still preserved in the Pennsylvania Hospital.

Most great anatomy books have been published as manuals for medical students, although the high cost of producing them meant that they were used as aids to teaching, seldom being owned by the students themselves. However, anatomy has always been of great interest to art students and artists, who need the knowledge of structure and surface anatomy to make convincing figures in sculpture or in painting. There were artists in the eighteenth century who carried out their own dissections and made anatomical drawings as studies to underpin their artistic activities, George Stubbs (1724–1806) famous for his paintings of horses, being the best known example. Most artists, however, looked to other sources for their information, and found, just as medical students did, that the anatomical atlases were too expensive to buy. A number of anatomical books began to be published aimed specifically at artists and this practice continued into the nineteenth and twentieth centuries. Giuseppe del Medico's book *Anatomia per Uso dei Pittori e Scultori*, 1811 (See plates 52–84) is one such. He may have acted as both draughtsman and engraver, and the result is a particularly elegant and yet entirely practical handbook. In 1833, Flaxman's *Anatomical Studies* was published posthumously in London 'for the use of artists'. It had some brief explanatory notes but consisted otherwise of drawings by Flaxman, engraved by Henry Landseer. It was modestly priced at £1,4 shillings. To realise how important this book was at the time one has to appreciate Flaxman's artistic status. He was born in 1755 and fifty years after his death in 1827, his statue was placed on the façade of Burlington House alongside Leonardo and other artistic giants. A Victorian comment on Flaxman described him as 'The Fra Angelico of Sculpture'. He studied at the Royal Academy School and as a student would have seen William Hunter lecture on anatomy there (see fig. v). Anatomy was a basic part of any art student's training but Flaxman continued these studies throughout his life. There is an early self portrait drawn when he was 23 which shows him with his hand on a skull, and it is known that he kept a skeleton in his studio throughout his career. As well as benefitting from the lectures of Hunter he was also in correspondence with the famous Edinburgh anatomist Alexander Munro.

Although Flaxman would not be considered today as ranking with Leonardo, his work still evokes more perfectly than that of any other artist the age of neo-classicism in England. He was, like Leonardo, very versatile. He was most famous at home for monumental and funerary sculpture, including monuments to Nelson and Lord Mansfield, but he also designed china for Wedgwood and silverware for Rundell and Bridge, many pieces being bought for the Royal Collection. On the Continent he was celebrated as a draughtsman who illustrated Homer, Dante and Aeschylus and his illustrated books achieved best-seller status.

What was remarkable about Flaxman's illustrations was their clear,

INTRODUCTION

concise quality which he managed to combine with a feeling of energy and spontaneity. The drawings depict figures and objects in outline only and these outlines combine clarity of construction with a surprising sense of abstraction. They are highly formalized and whilst being extremely spare, they look fully realised. There are no superfluous lines or dashing strokes but they are nevertheless lively. Flaxman's drawings have been described as 'done with minimal means; his outlines combine the briskness of the first thought with the care and delicacy of the most consummate finish'.

The economy of form which characterizes Flaxman's drawing depended on a system of abstraction and he articulated surfaces so that there is interplay between the simplified forms in his drawings and the spaces which surround them. Flaxman's illustrations had enormous influence throughout Europe. He received many of the artistic accolades of his time, being elected a Royal Academician and in 1810 being appointed as the first Professor of Sculpture at the Royal Academy. Flaxman saw this as the peak of his official recognition and in the six lectures he was required to give each year he made a pioneering attempt, as a British sculptor, to speak about his art.

Most of Flaxman's anatomy drawings are contained in three sketchbooks now in the Fitzwilliam Museum in Cambridge. They have a clarity and linear precision which is very similar to his illustrations but there is some use made of tone on the skeleton drawings and the drawings of muscles sometimes use freely drawn parallel lines to describe muscular form and tension. The introduction to the book states 'these exhibitions of muscular mechanism' were made by Flaxman 'for his own use and instruction' and this, the introduction continues, gives them 'a practical recommendation superior to all critical eulogy'.

The final work illustrated in this selection is Gray's *Anatomy*, probably the best known of all anatomical manuals. First published in 1858, it has long played a major role in the education of medical students. The illustrations by H. Vandyke Carter are beautifully executed, clear and diagramatic, setting the style for modern text books, with their emphasis on precision and science rather than art.

Ian Simpson

Fig v
Johann Zoffany, *William Hunter giving an anatomy lesson at the Royal Academy*, *c*.1775, oil
on canvas. Photograph: Royal College of Physicians.
Anatomy lessons at the Academy would have entailed drawing from the usually nude model,
as well as being taught about the body's underlying structure using the skeleton seen here and
also textbooks produced specifically for artists. Joshua Reynolds, first President of the
Academy, can be seen with an ear trumpet.

THE PLATES

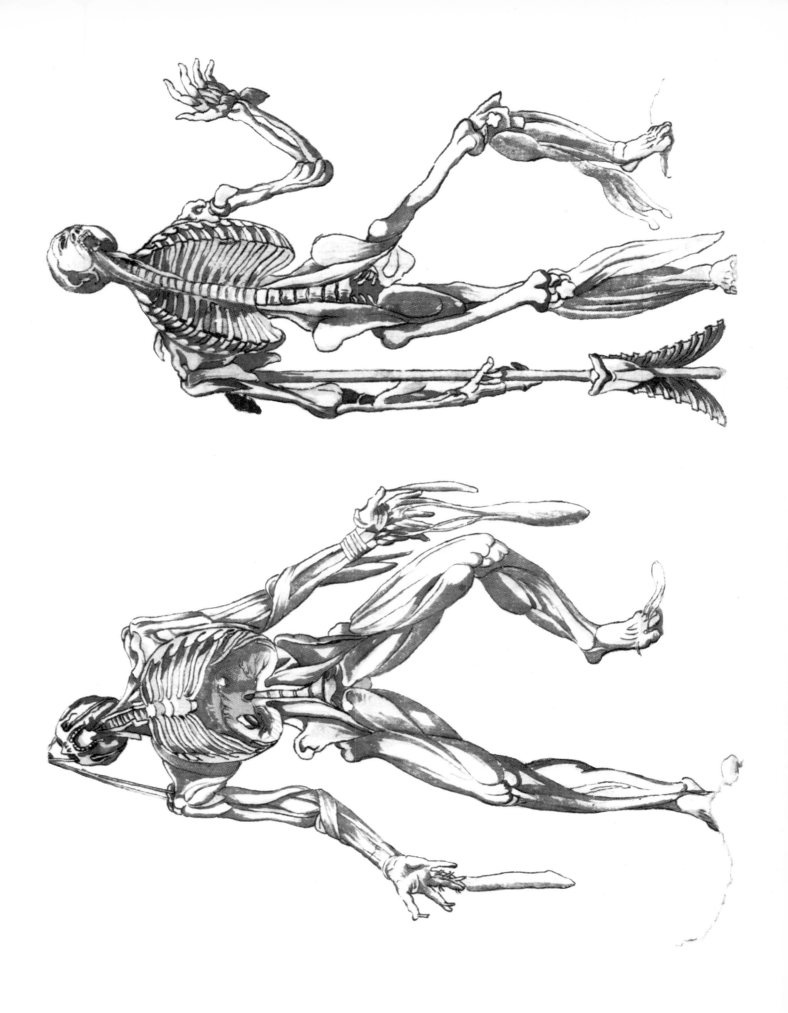

PLATE 1
ANDREAS VESALIUS, *De Humani Corporis Fabrica*, 1543. Photograph: Victoria & Albert
Museum. Pen and ink drawing by an unknown artist, possibly Jan Stephan Kalkar, for
Vesalius' book. The drawing would have been made into a woodcut for reproduction. The
flayed figures here, posed by means of ropes, are taken from actual corpses.

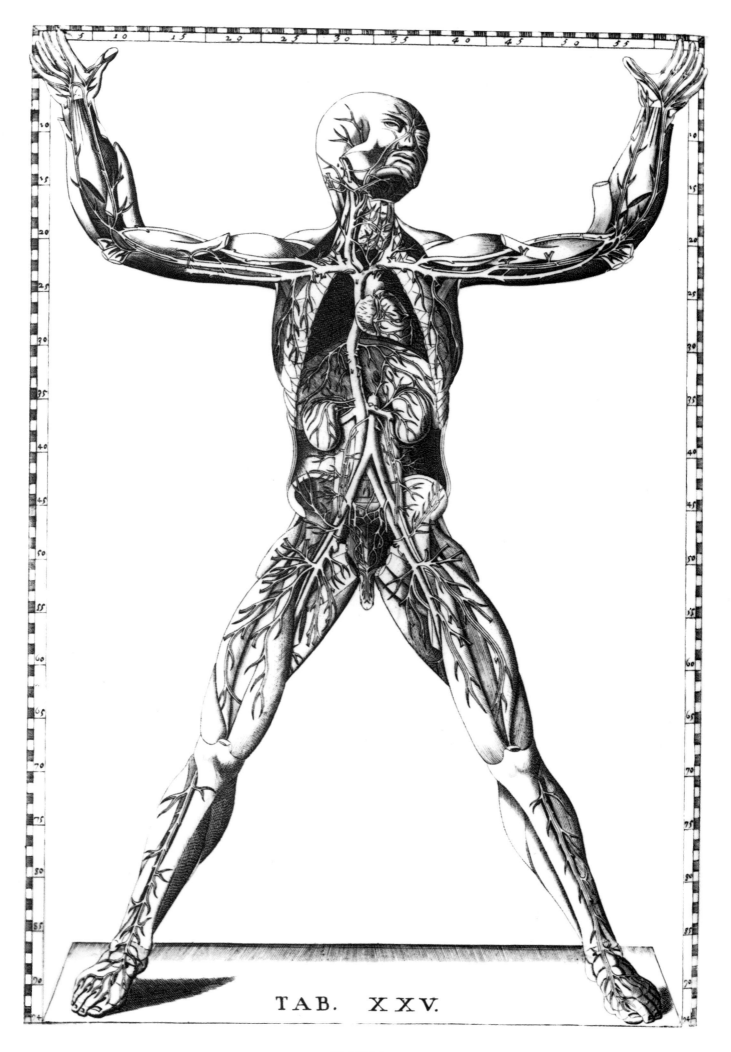

TAB. XXV.

PLATE 2

BARTOLOMEO EUSTACHIO, *Tabulae Anatomicae Clarissimi Viri*, ed. Lancisi, 1714, Plate XXV. Engraved by Giulio de Musi after a drawing possibly by Eustachio himself, or his relative and assistant Matteo Pinio, *c.*1552. Photograph: British Museum. Front view of a standing male figure showing the major blood vessels of the body. Each figure is enclosed by an unusual frame which is divided into segments and numbered in order to allow specific areas to be identified by a 'grid-reference'.

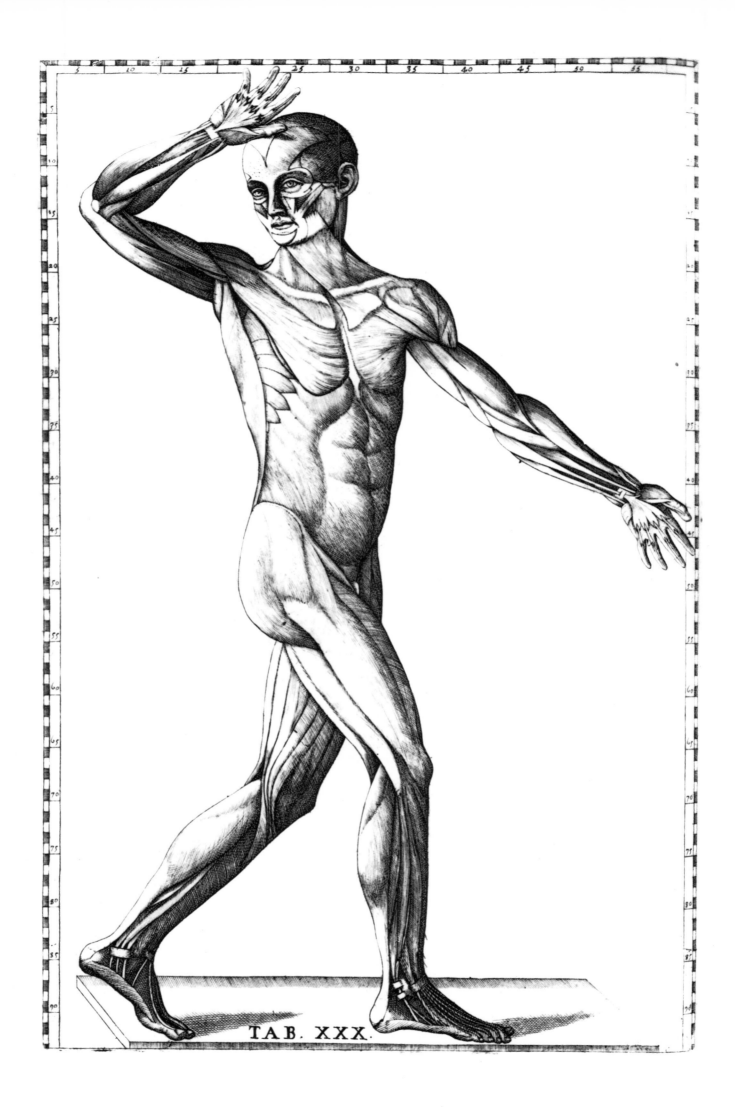

TAB. XXX.

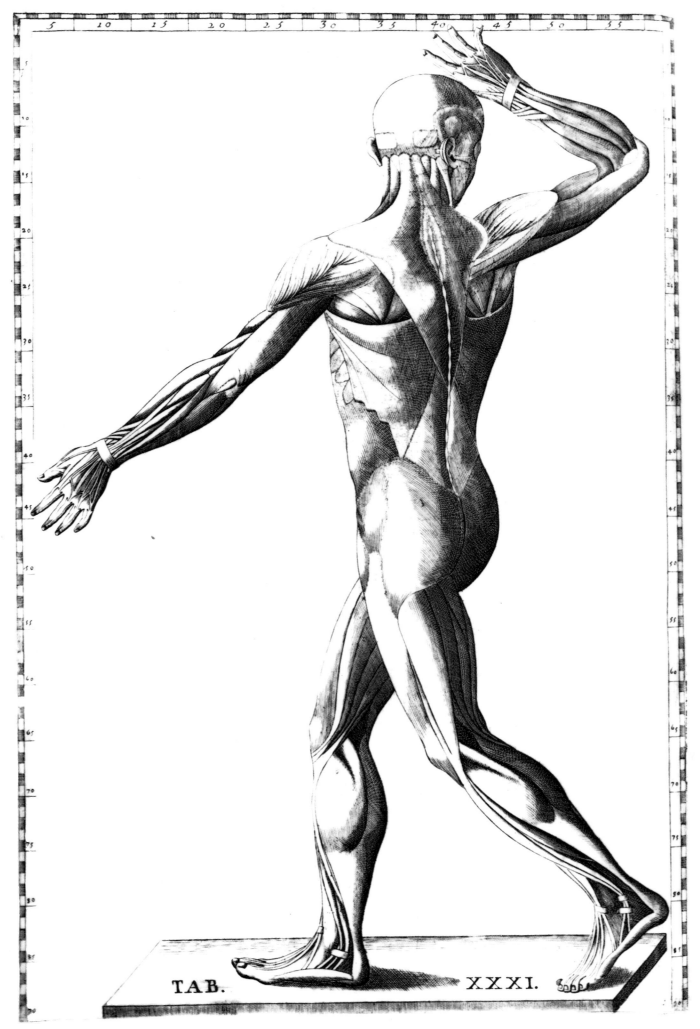

TAB.   XXXI.

PLATES 3 & 4

BARTOLOMEO EUSTACHIO, *Tabulae Anatomicae Clarissimi Viri*, ed. Lancisi, 1714, Plates XXX and XXXI.
Engraved by Giulio de Musi after drawings by Eustachio or Pinio, *c*.1552. Photograph: British Museum. This
pair of figures showing the muscular structure of the front and back of the body is one of five pairs which reveal
each layer of muscles until, finally, the skeleton itself is reached.

OSTEOGRAPHIA OR
THE ANATOMY OF THE BONES
(1733)
and
ANATOMY OF THE HUMANE BODY
(1712)

by

William Cheselden

Artist: unknown

Photographs: British Museum

William Cheselden was surgeon to Her Majesty Queen Anne, a Fellow of the Royal Society, member of the Royal Academy of Surgery in Paris and surgeon at St. Thomas's Hospital, London. Apart from this information, however, little is known of the author of the two works reproduced here, or of the artist responsible for the drawings. It is said that the title page of *Osteographia* (see opposite) shows Cheselden making a drawing of a skeleton using a *camera obscura*. All of the illustrations were supposed to have been made using this device.

OSTEOGRAPHIA,
OR THE
ANATOMY
OF THE
BONES.

BY WILLIAM CHESELDEN

SURGEON TO HER ·MAJESTY;

F. R. S.

SURGEON TO St THOMAS'S HOSPITAL,

AND MEMBER OF THE ROYAL ACADEMY OF SURGERY AT PARIS.

LONDON MDCCXXXIII.

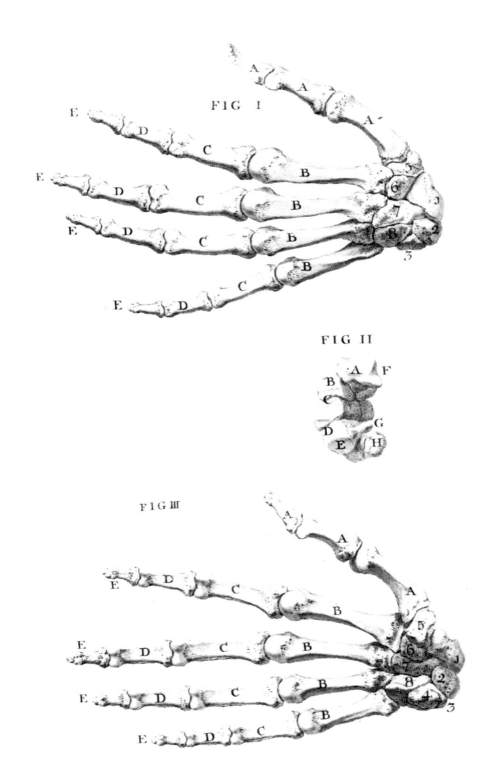

PLATE 6

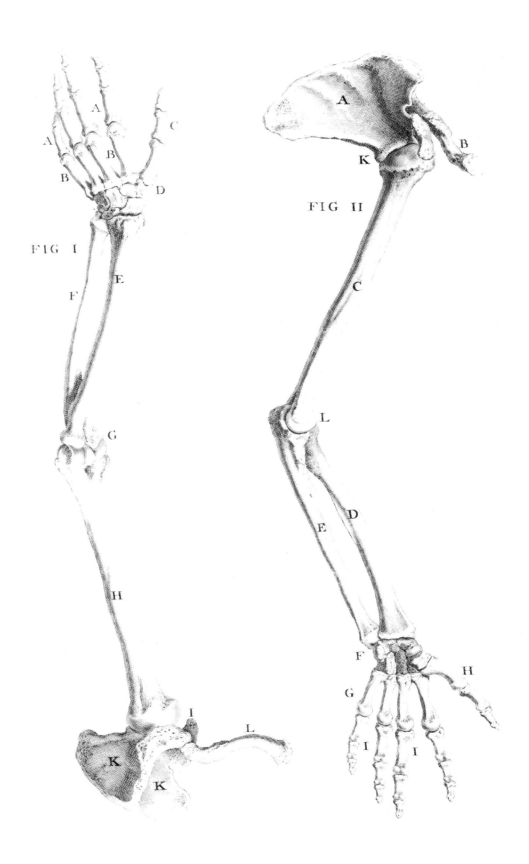

PLATE 7

WILLIAM CHESELDEN, *Osteographia*, 1733, Plate XXVI. 'Fig. I The outside of the scapula,
arm and hand. Fig. II The inside of the scapula, arm and hand.'

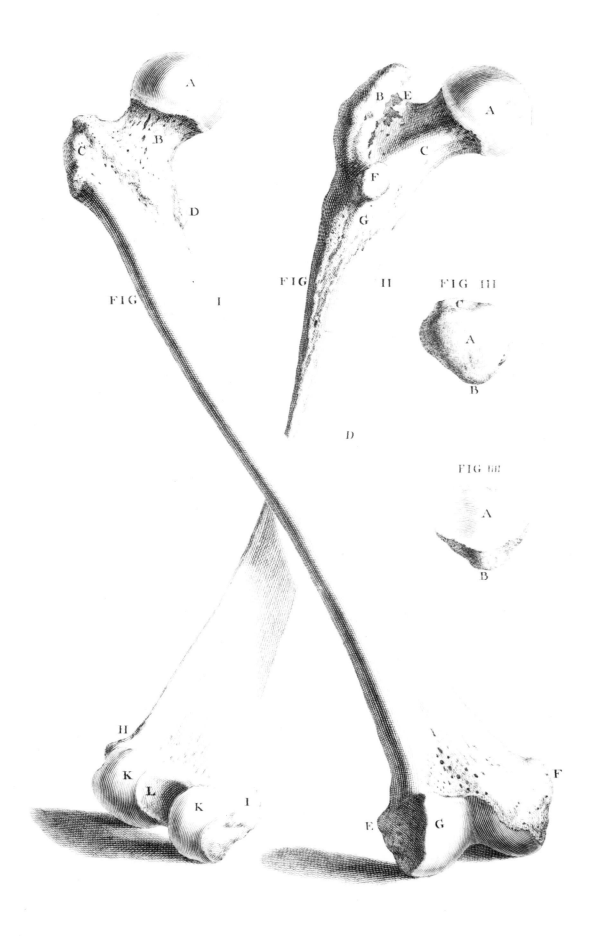

PLATE 8

WILLIAM CHESELDEN, *Osteographia*, 1733, Plate XXVII. 'Fig. I The foreside of the os
femoris [thighbone]. Fig. II The backside of the os femoris. Fig. III The foreside of the
patella [kneecap]. Fig. IIII The under side of the patella, which moves upon the os femoris.'

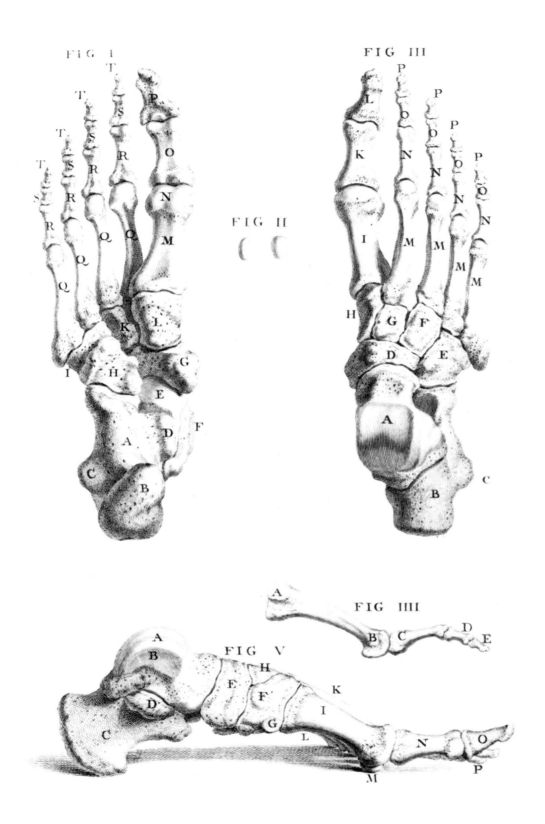

PLATE 9

WILLIAM CHESELDEN, *Osteographia*, 1733, Plate XXIX. 'Fig. I The under side of the
bones of the foot. Fig. II The sesamoid bones of the great toe. Fig. III The upper side of the
bones of the foot. Fig. IIII The side (next to the great toe) of the bones of the second toe.
Fig. V The inside of the bones of the foot.'

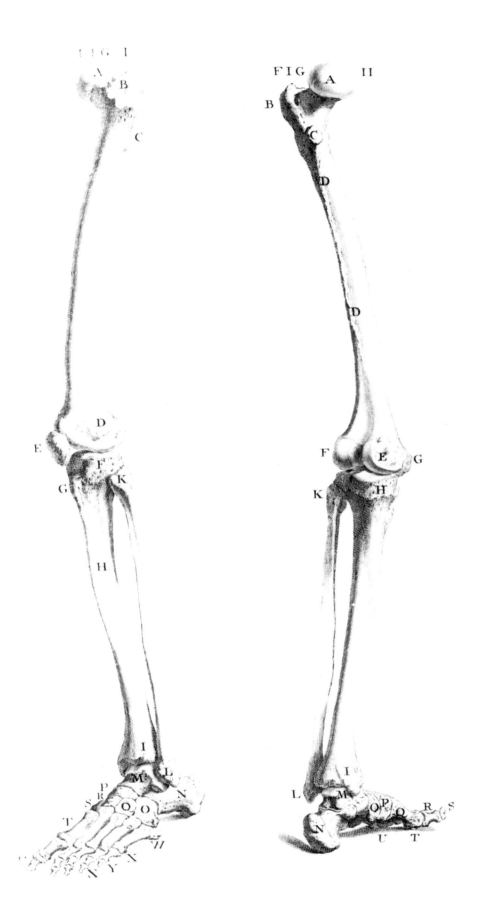

PLATE 10
WILLIAM CHESELDEN, *Osteographia*, 1733, Plate XXX. 'Fig. I The outside of the bones of
the lower limb. Fig. II The inside of the bones of the lower limb.'

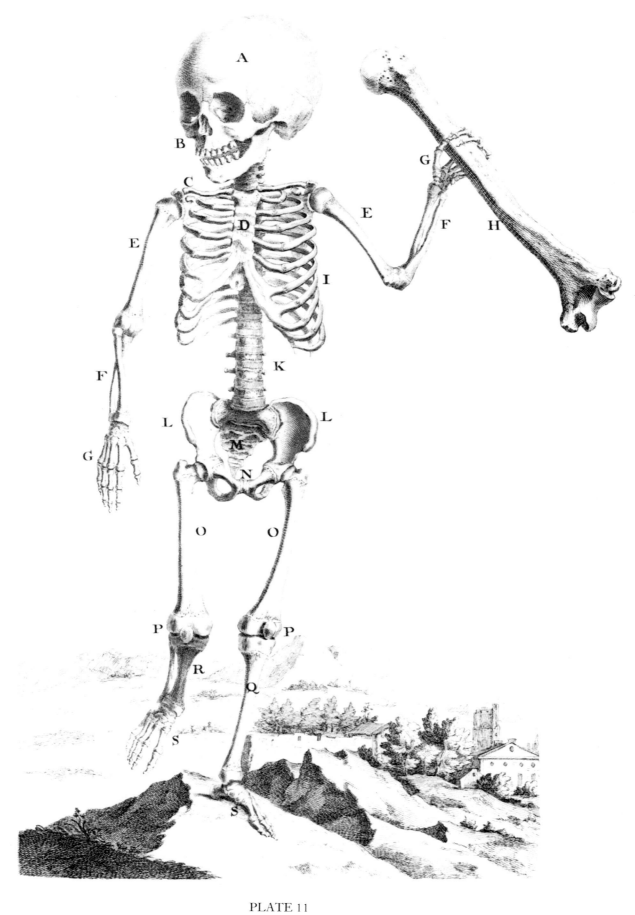

PLATE 11

WILLIAM CHESELDEN, *Osteographia*, 1733, Plate XXXII. 'Fig. I The skeleton of a child a
year and a half old, with the os humeris [upper arm bone] of a man in the left hand, to show
by comparison the size of the child; here also are to be observed the different shapes and
textures of the several bones.'

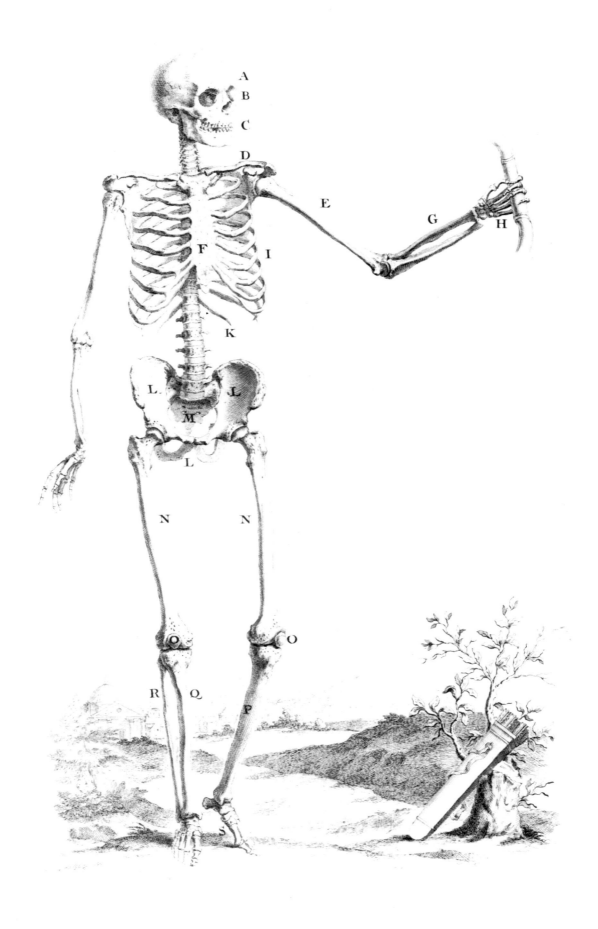

PLATE 12

WILLIAM CHESELDEN, *Osteographia*, 1733, Plate XXXV. 'The skeleton of a man, in the same proportions and attitude with the Belvedere Apollo.' The skeleton is seen against a classical landscape to reinforce the allusion to one of the most famous classical Roman statues.

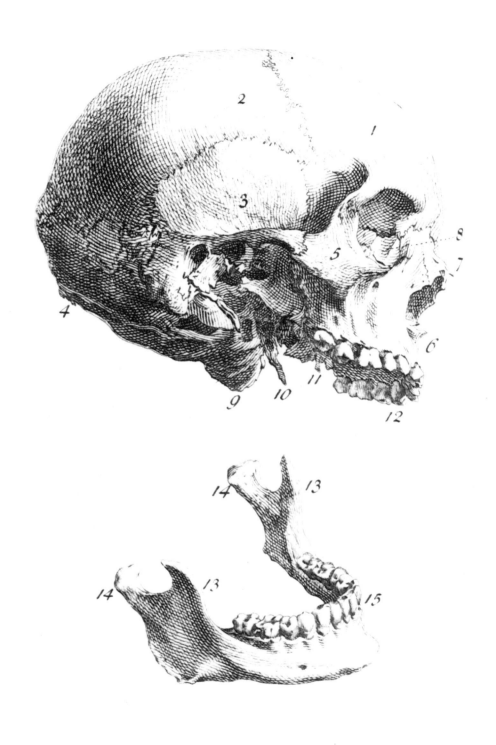

PLATE 13
WILLIAM CHESELDEN, *Anatomy of the Humane Body*, 1712, Table II. Skull and, detached,
the jawbone with the various elements numbered for identification.

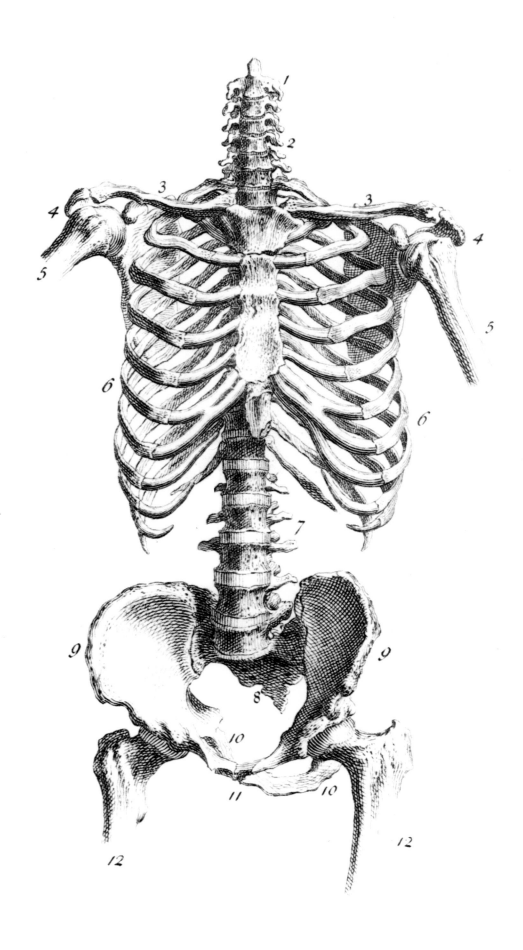

PLATE 14
WILLIAM CHESELDEN, *Anatomy of the Humane Body*, 1712, Plate IV. Truncated skeleton.
The pelvis is turned slightly in order to darken the shadow on the right-hand side and so
appear more three-dimensional.

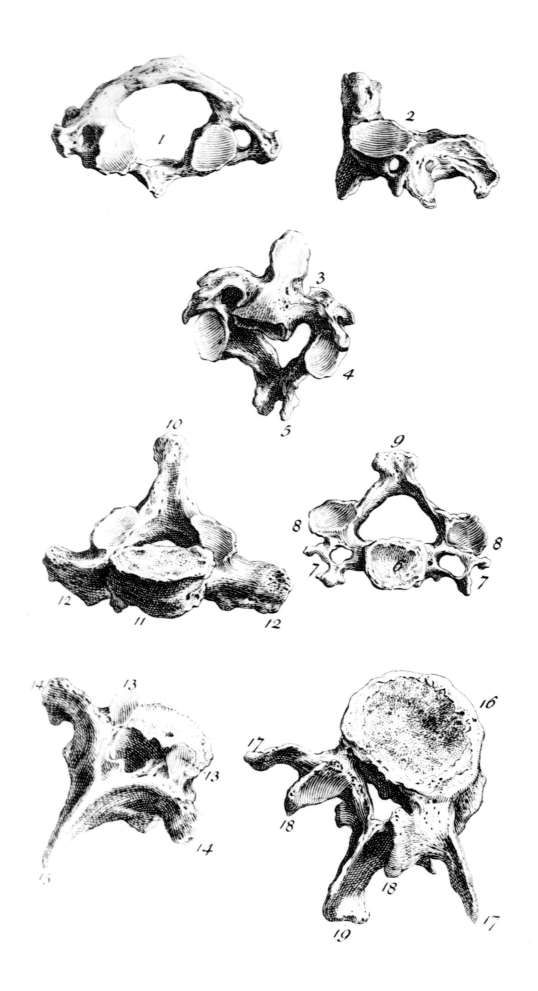

PLATE 15
William Cheselden, *Anatomy of the Humane Body*, 1712, Table V. These studies of the
different vertebrae make skilful use of different bone textures.

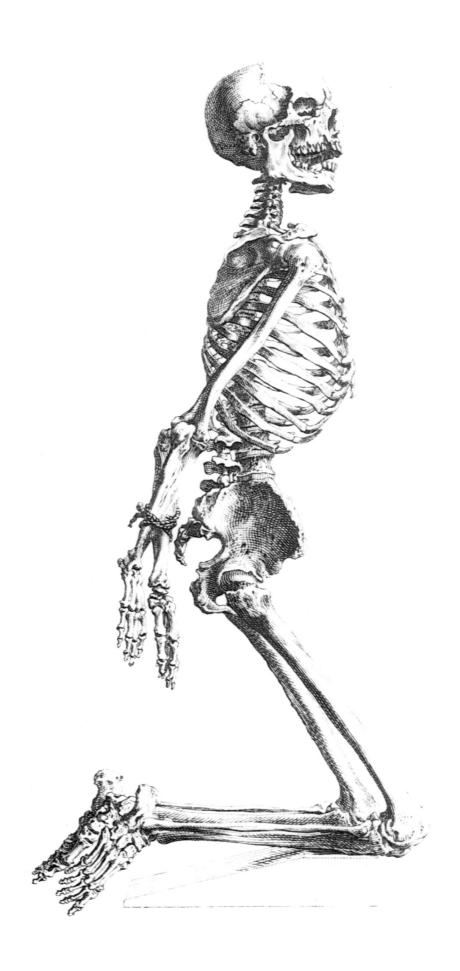

PLATE 16

WILLIAM CHESELDEN, *Anatomy of The Humane Body*, 1712, Table X. 'A skeleton was put
into this posture to shew it in a greater scale. It was thought better not to figure it, all these
bones being explained in former plates, and the design of this being to shew them together
without being defaced with references.'

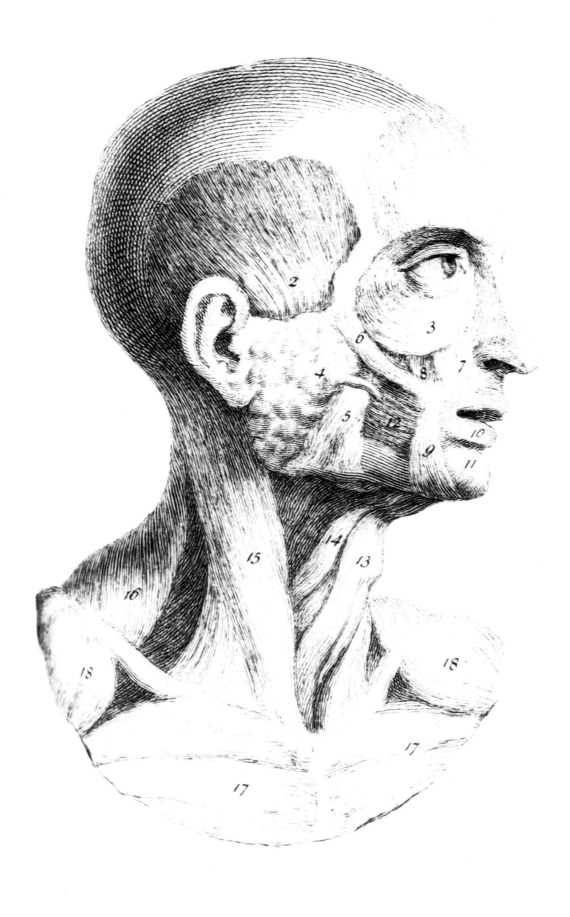

PLATE 17

WILLIAM CHESELDEN, *Anatomy of the Humane Body*, 1712, Table XI. The muscles of the face and neck. The style of engraving changes to depict the muscles and is much freer, with the lines following the form of the muscle. The head is cut off at the shoulders in much the same way as a classical bust.

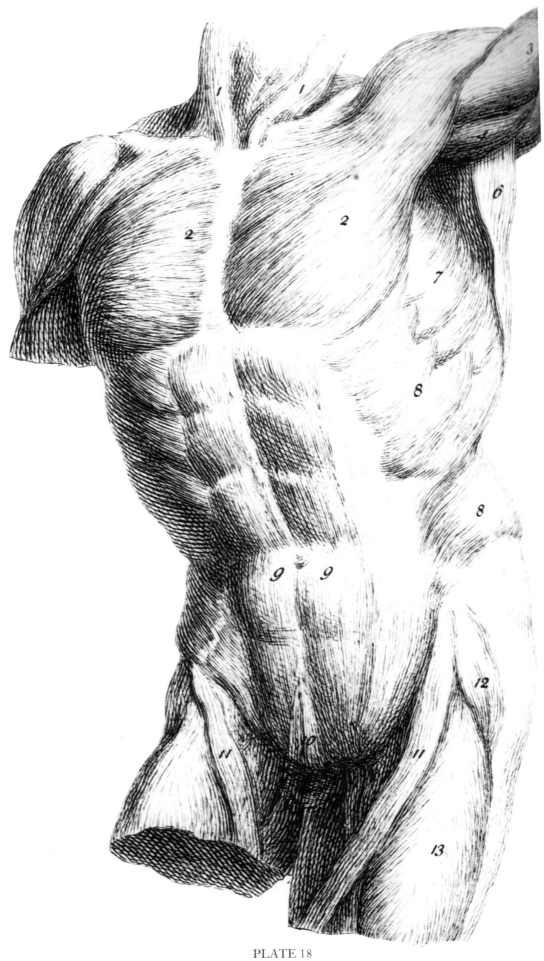

PLATE 18

WILLIAM CHESELDEN, *Anatomy of the Humane Body*, 1733, Table XII. The muscles of the
torso seen from the front. The figure is posed like a truncated Roman statue. It is interesting
to compare this treatment with that of Eustachio (see Plate 3).

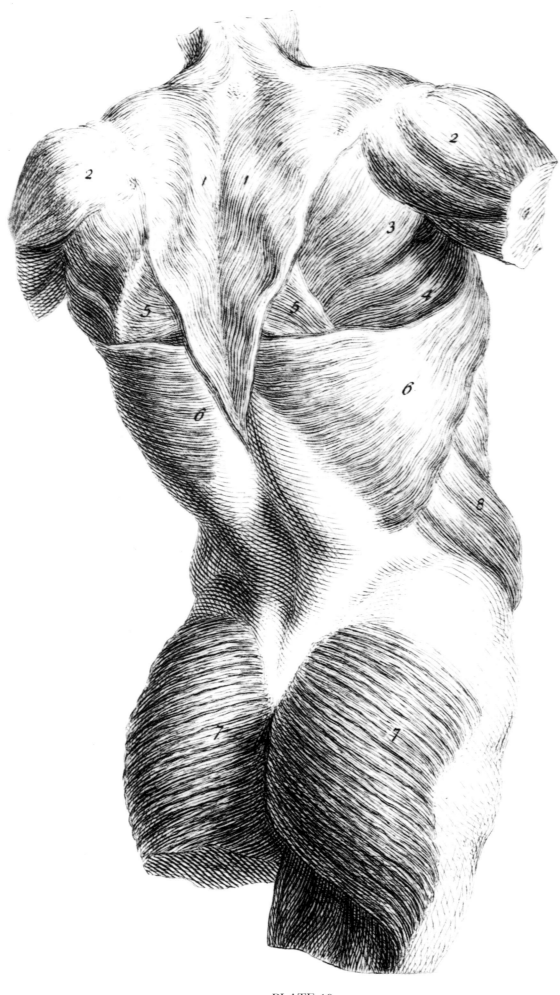

PLATE 19

WILLIAM CHESELDEN, *Anatomy of the Humane Body*, 1712, Table XIII. The muscles of the torso seen from the back.

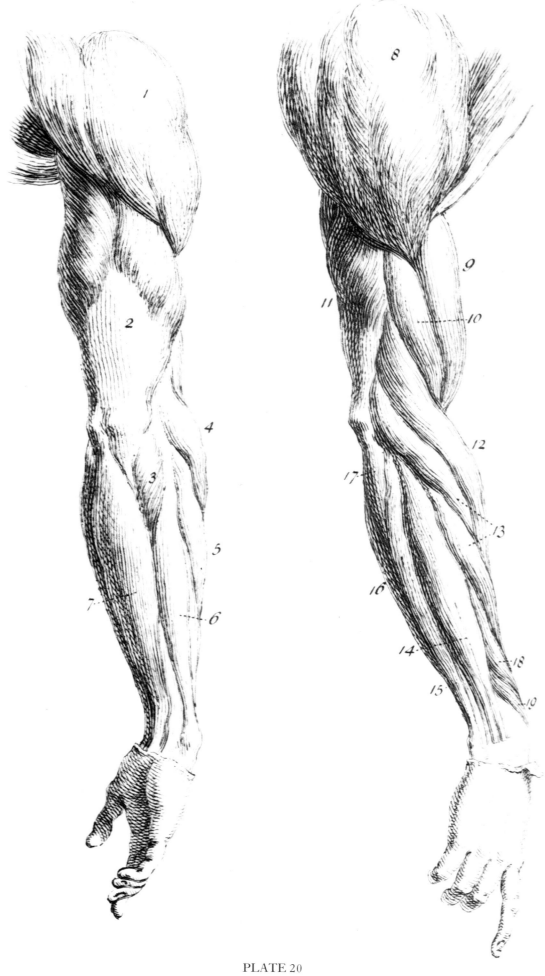

PLATE 20

WILLIAM CHESELDEN, *Anatomy of the Humane Body*, 1712, Table XIV. The muscles of the
inside and outside of the arm. Something can be deduced of the dissection techniques used
from the way in which the skin is left like a glove on the hand and wrist.

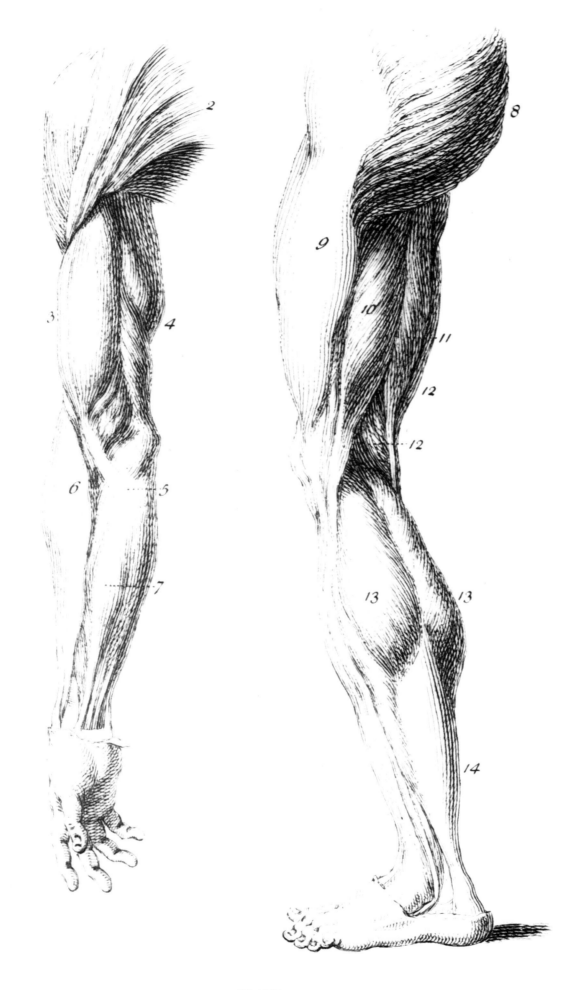

PLATE 21
Wɪʟʟɪᴀᴍ Cʜᴇsᴇʟᴅᴇɴ, *Anatomy of the Humane Body*, 1712, Table XV. The muscles of the
side of the arm and the back of the leg.

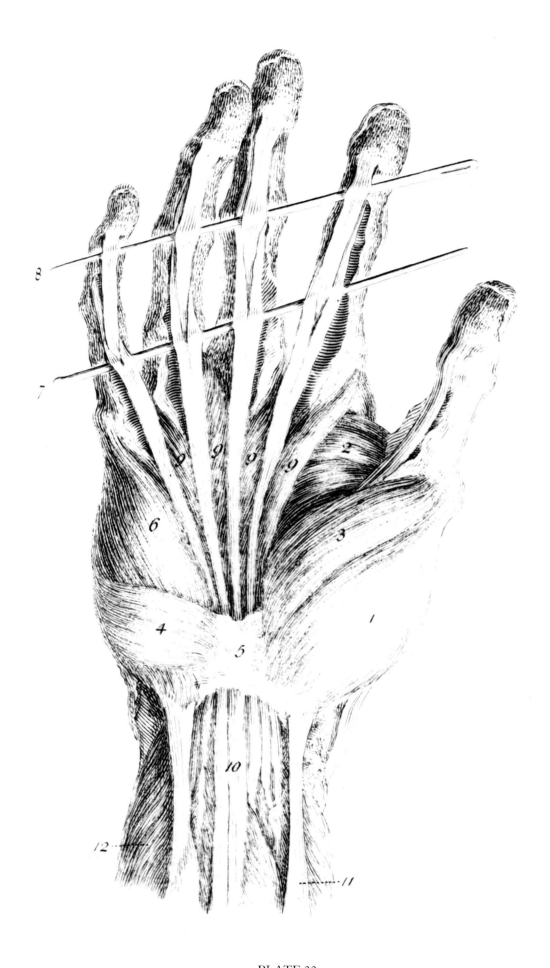

PLATE 22

WILLIAM CHESELDEN, *Anatomy of the Humane Body*, 1712, Table XVII. The muscles of the
hand. It is interesting to compare this illustration with that of the same subject by Blandin,
(Plate 85) and by Gray (Plate 117).

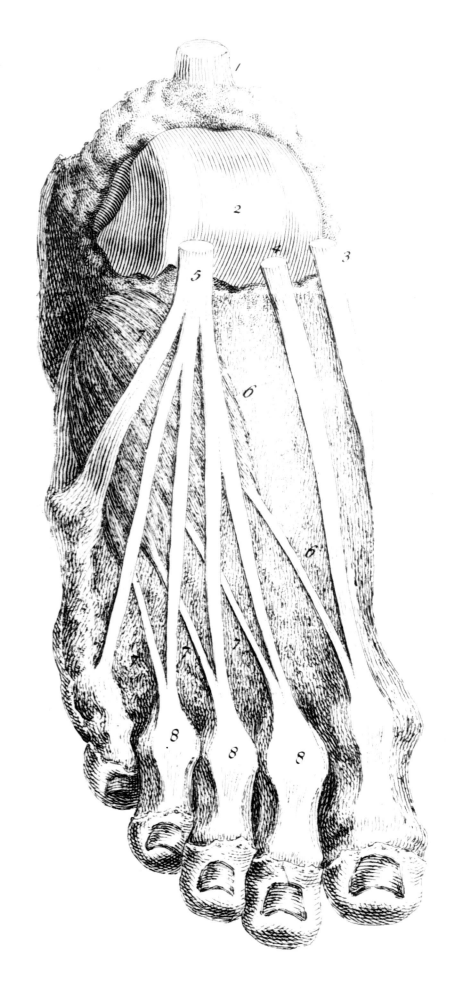

PLATE 23
WILLIAM CHESELDEN, *Anatomy of the Humane Body*, 1712, Table XVIII. The muscles of
the foot.

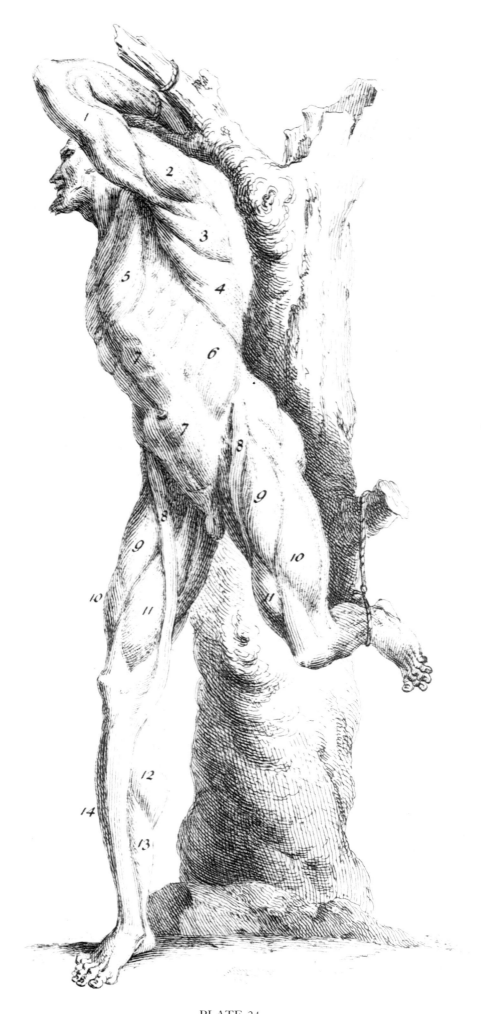

PLATE 24

WILLIAM CHESELDEN, *Anatomy of the Humane Body*, 1712, Table XIX. The major muscles of the body are shown in this figure tied to a tree in the pose of Marsyas.

PLATE 25

WILLIAM CHESELDEN, *Anatomy of the Humane Body*, 1712, Table XX. 'This table is done after the famous statue of Hercules and Antaeus. The muscles here are exhibited being all explained in the other plates, the figures are omitted to preserve the beauty of the plate.'

TABULAE SCELETI ET MUSCULORUM CORPORIS HUMANI (1747)

by

Bernhard Siegfried Albinus

Artist: J. Wandelaar

Photographs: British Museum

Albinus was a pioneer of a new epoch of human anatomy, producing work of extreme thoroughness and great exactitude. He believed that drawings should not be made freehand but from actual measurements and not from one body but from data collected from several bodies to make a composite figure so that "actual truth will be displayed." His illustrator Wandelaar produced both drawings and engravings and although Albinus spoke highly of him, he treated the artist "as a tool", a craftsman who would painstakingly carry out his tasks for him.

Camper (see plates 42–44) criticized the first twelve plates in the book because he found the backgrounds irrelevant. Wandelaar had attempted to emphasise the figures by placing them against a dark background; these unusual settings are surely the most attractive feature to modern eyes.

The engraving contains the following text within it:

BERN·SIEGF·ALBINI
TABVLAE·ANATOMICAE
MVSCVLORVM
HOMINIS

PLATE 26

BERNHARD ALBINUS, *Tabulae Sceleti et Musculorum Corporis Humani*, 1747, Tabula I.
Drawn and engraved by J. Wandelaar. Figure showing the body's first layer of muscles seen
against a classical background.

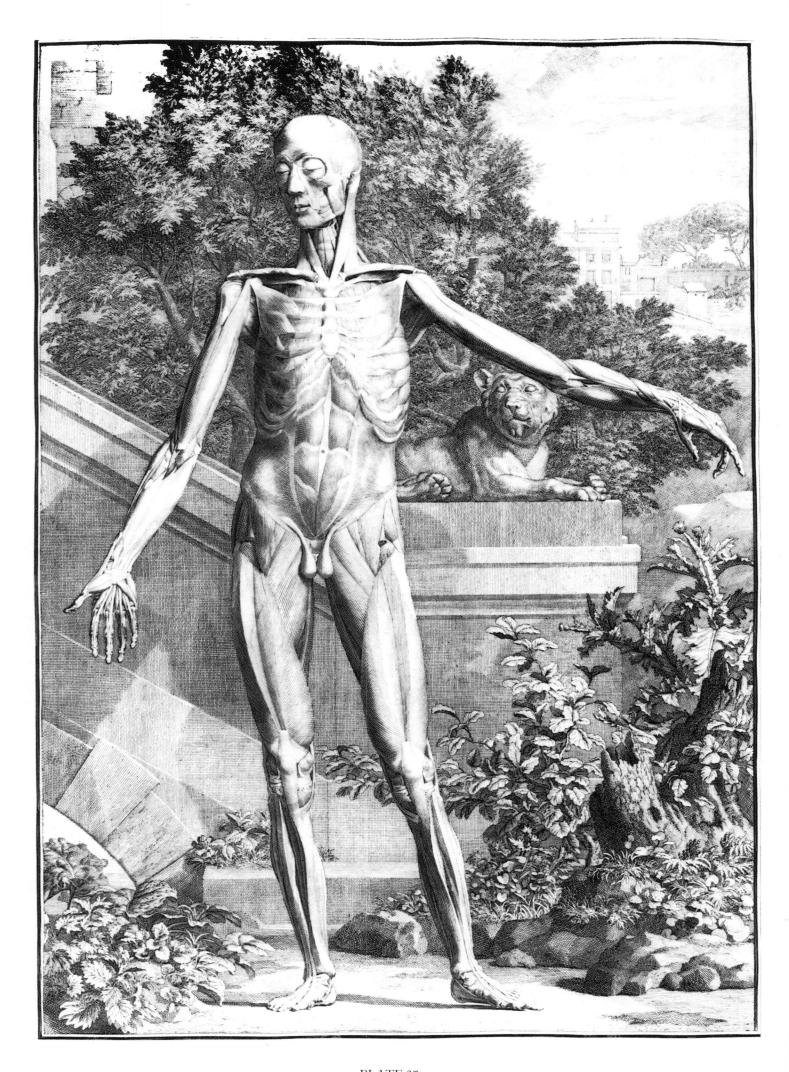

PLATE 27
BERNHARD ALBINUS, *Tabulae Sceleti*, 1747, Tabula II. Drawn and engraved by
J. Wandelaar. Figure showing the body's second layer of muscles, again seen against a
classical background with several architectural features.

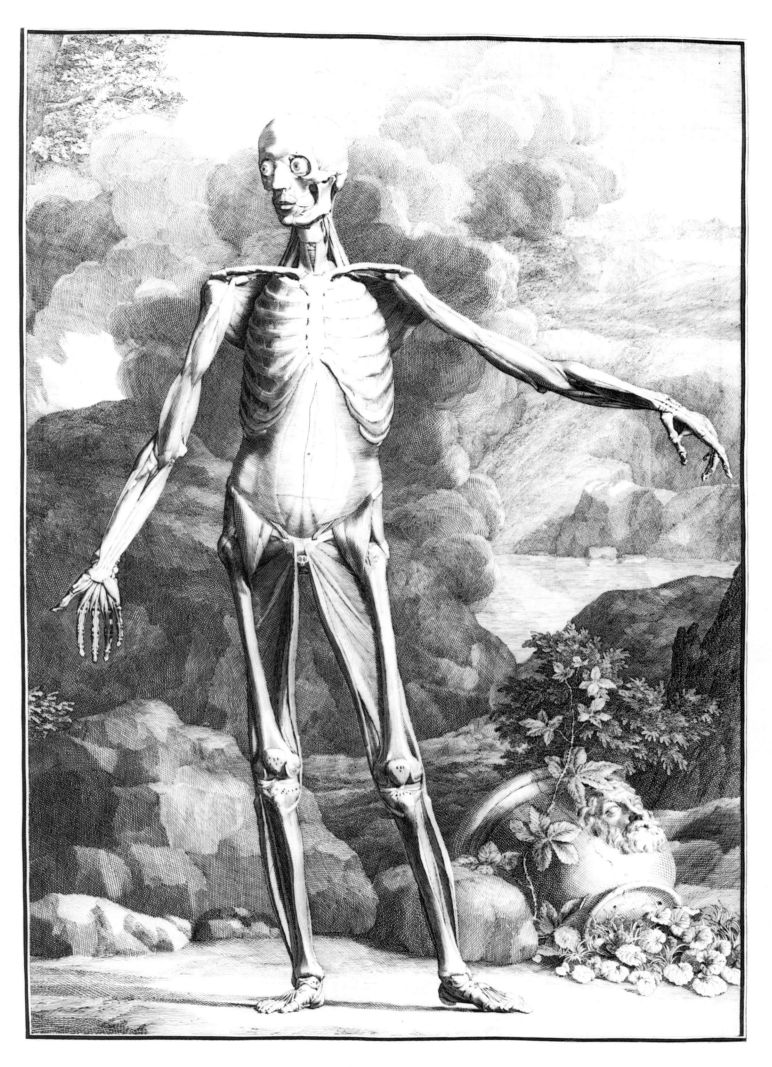

PLATE 28
BERNHARD ALBINUS, *Tabulae Sceleti*, 1747, Tabula III. Drawn and engraved by
J. Wandelaar. Figure showing the body's third layer of muscles; the background this time is
mountainous and includes a smoking volcano.

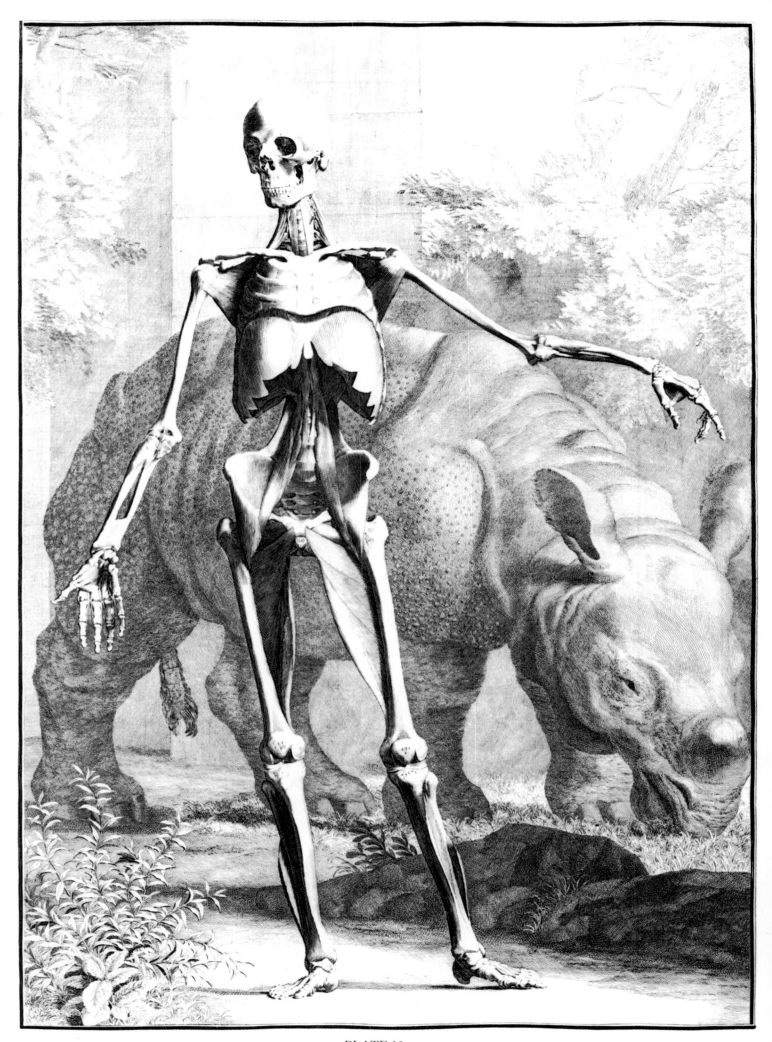

PLATE 29
BERNHARD ALBINUS, *Tabulae Sceleti*, 1747, Tabula IV. Drawn and engraved by
J. Wandelaar. Figure showing the body's last layer of muscles, stripped down almost to the
skeleton. The figure is posed against a rhinoceros, not, one imagines, a common sight in
eighteenth century Holland.

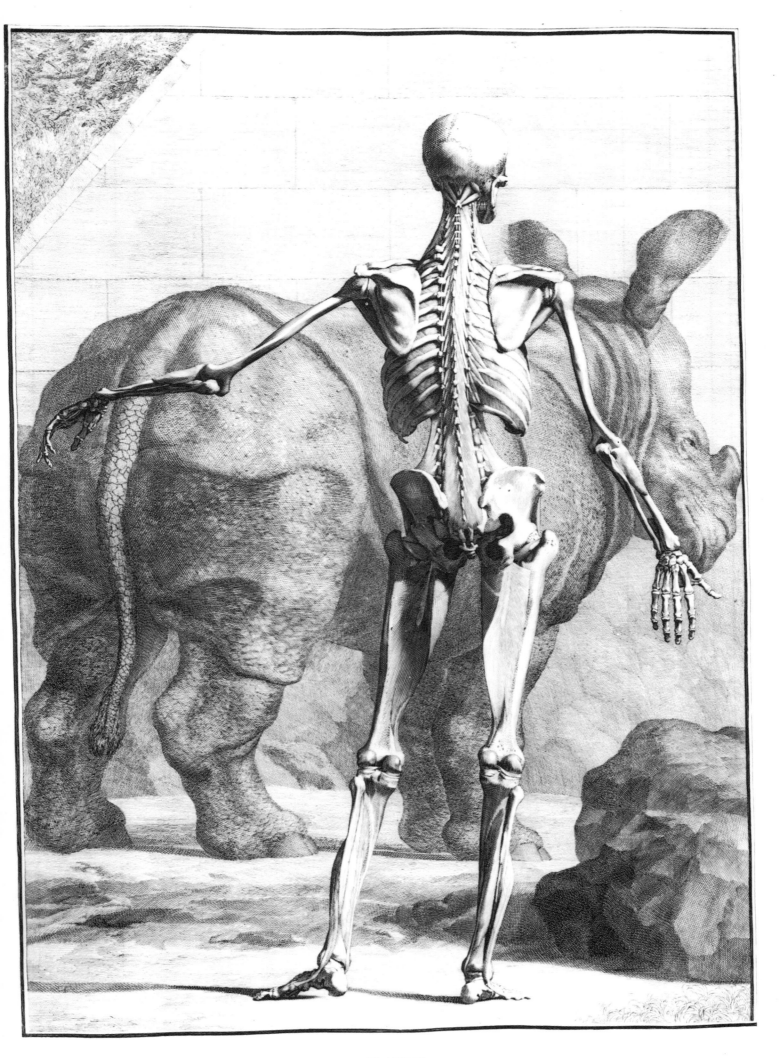

PLATE 30

BERNHARD ALBINUS, *Tabulae Sceleti*, 1747, Tabula VIII. Drawn and engraved by
J. Wandelaar. The 'pair' to the figure in Plate 29, this time seen from the back, and again
posed against a rhinoceros, also seen from behind!

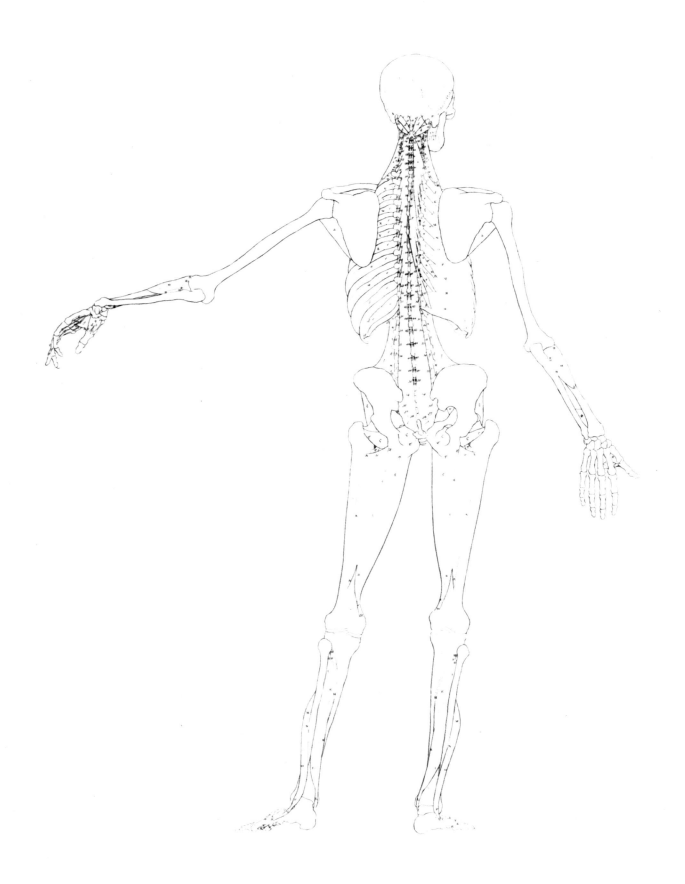

PLATE 31
BERNHARD ALBINUS, *Tabulae Sceleti*, 1747, Tabula VIII. Drawn and engraved by
J. Wandelaar. This outline figure is the key to Plate 30. Similar figures accompany all the
illustrations (Plates 26–30) in order to identify the various muscles without having to impair
the beauty of the engraving by putting numbers on it.

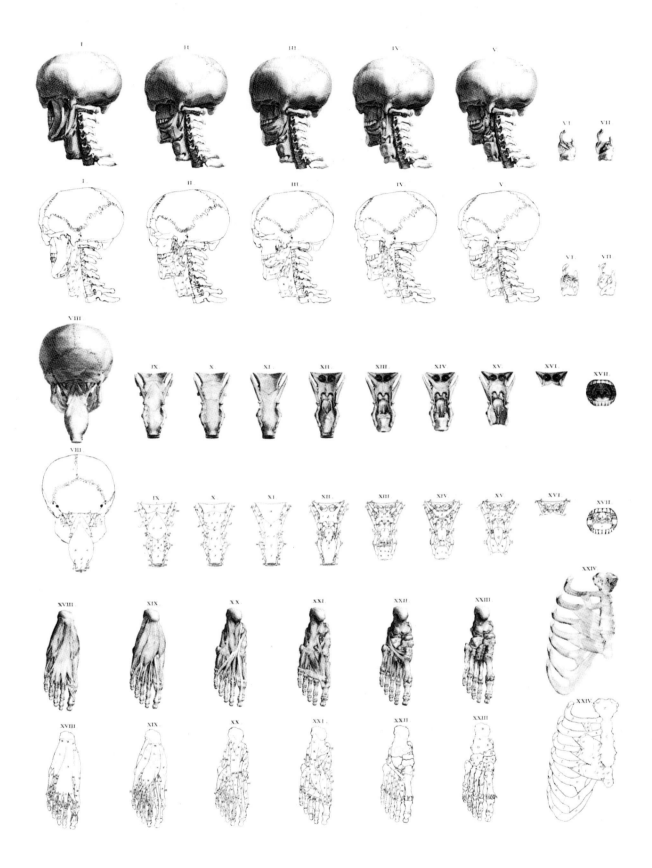

PLATE 32

BERNHARD ALBINUS, *Tabulae Sceleti*, 1747, Tabula X. Drawn and engraved by
J. Wandelaar. Detailed drawings of the skull, neck, feet and rib cage. Like the previous
engravings showing the whole figure, each 'layer' is shown and is successively stripped away.
Each stage is accompanied by an outline drawing below it which explains what is depicted.

SETT OF ANATOMICAL TABLES
(1754)

by

William Smellie

Artist: Jan Van Rymsdyk

Engraved by Charles Grignion

Photographs: British Museum

Smellie's pioneering work on gynaecology and childbirth, controversial in his day, was disseminated by means of this book, which was translated into a number of languages and was regarded as a 'bible' until well into the nineteenth century.

GRAVID UTERUS (1774)

by

William Hunter

Artist: Jan Van Rymsdyk

Engraved by Canot & Ravenet

Photographs: British Museum

These plates were made from the dissection of a woman who died suddenly in the end of her ninth month of pregnancy, in the year 1750.

NATURAL HISTORY OF THE
HUMAN TEETH (1771)

by

John Hunter

Original chalk drawings by Jan Van Rymsdyk

Photographs: Royal College of Surgeons

These drawings were made under the direction of John Hunter, brother of William (see above).

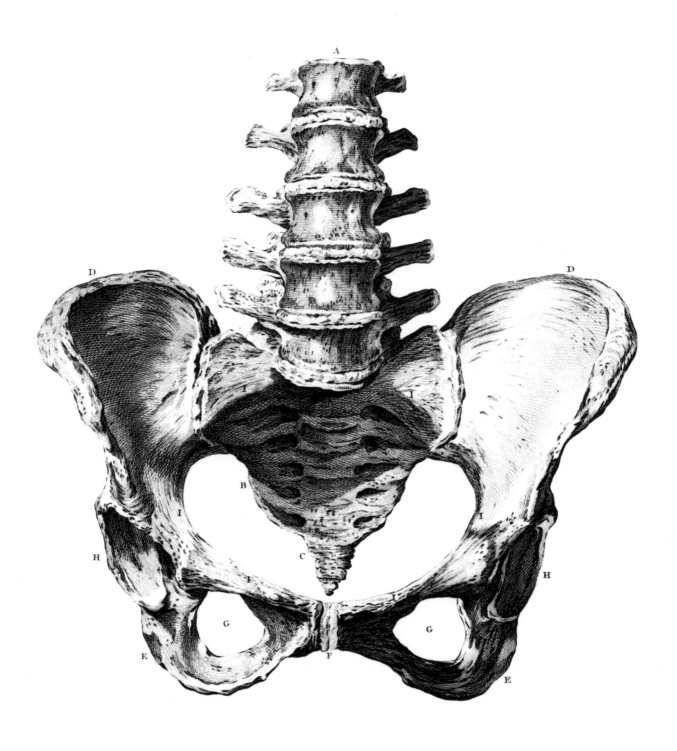

PLATE 33

WILLIAM SMELLIE, *Sett of Anatomical Tables*, 1754, Table I. Drawn by Jan van Rymsdyk
and engraved by Charles Grignion. The 'First Table represents in a front-view the bones of a
well formed *pelvis*.' Smellie's pioneering work in gynaecology and childbirth, controversial
in his day, was disseminated through this book which was translated into a number of
languages and was regarded as a 'bible' until well into the nineteenth century.

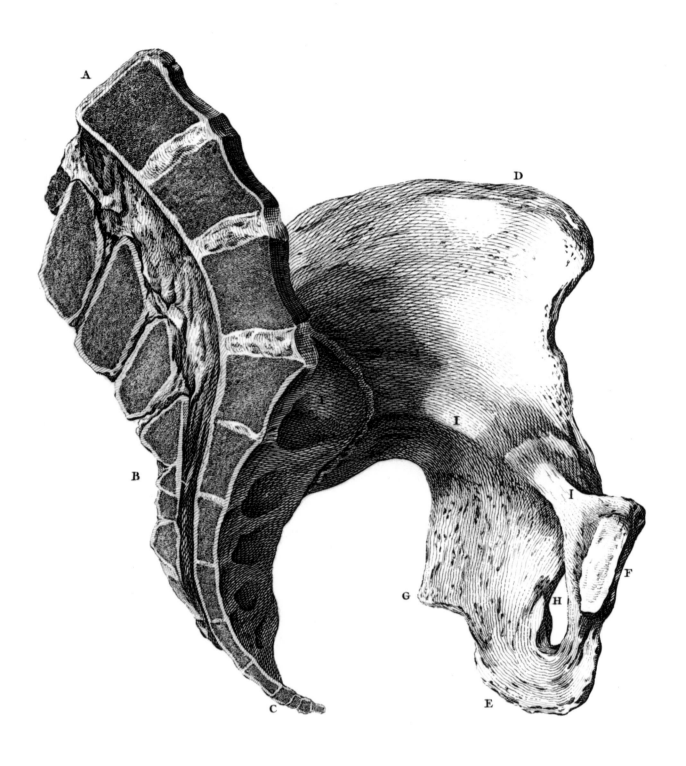

PLATE 34

WILLIAM SMELLIE, *Sett of Anatomical Tables*, 1754, Table II. Drawn by Jan van Rymsdyk and engraved by Charles Grignion. The 'Second Table gives a lateral and internal view of the *pelvis*, the same being divided longitudinally.'

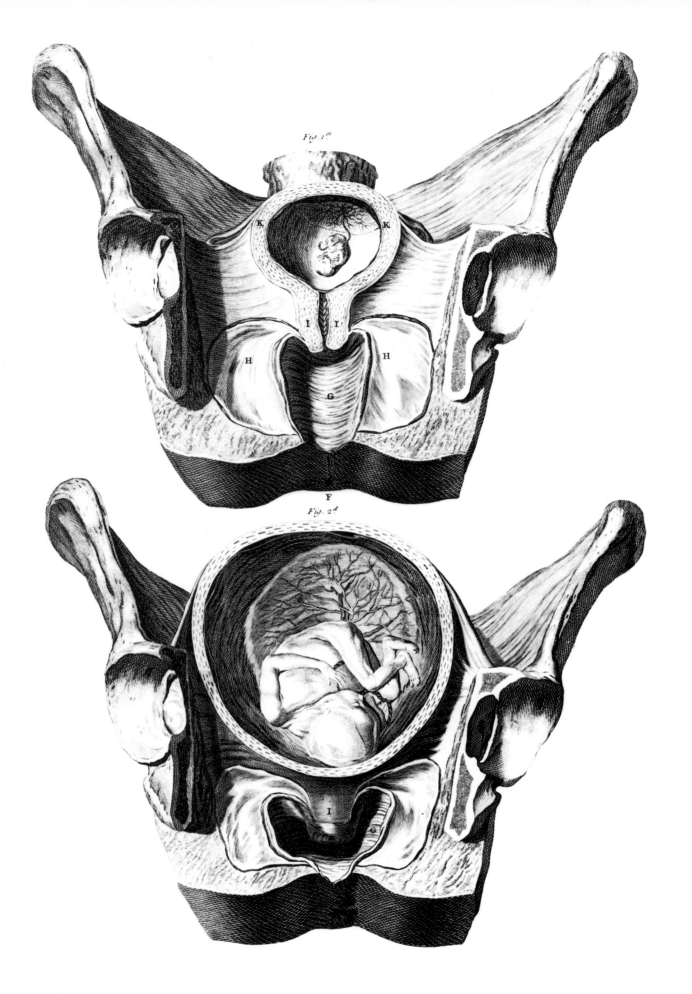

PLATE 35

WILLIAM SMELLIE, *Sett of Anatomical Tables*, 1754, Table VI. Drawn by Jan van Rymsdyk
and engraved by Charles Grignion. The 'Sixth Table Figure I . . . shews the *uterus* as it
appears in the second or third month of pregnancy, its anterior part being here likewise
removed. Figure II represents the *uterus* in the fourth or fifth month of pregnancy in the same
view and section of the parts with the former figure.'

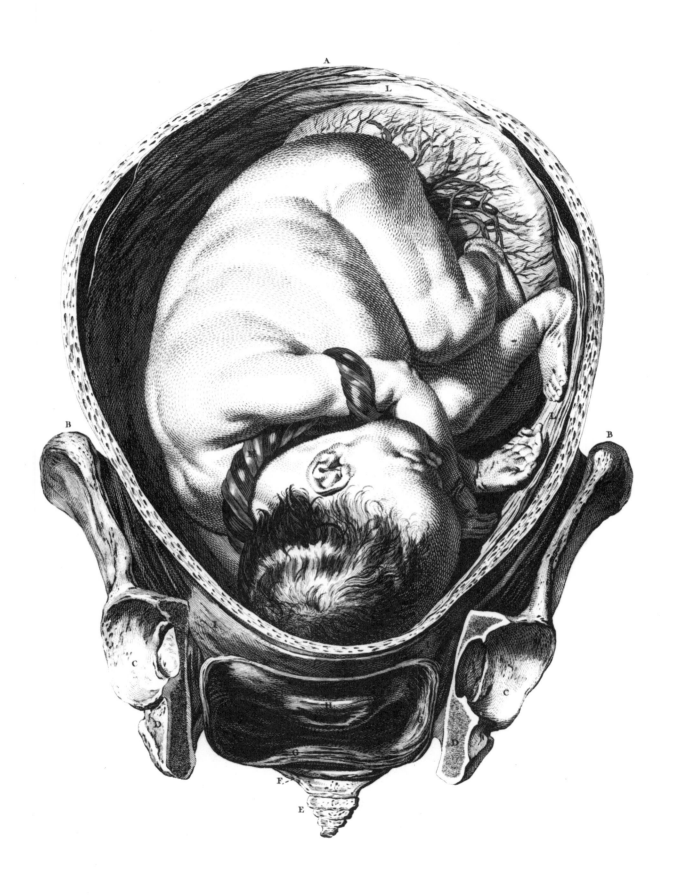

PLATE 36

WILLIAM SMELLIE, *Sett of Anatomical Tables*, 1754, Table IX. Drawn by Jan van Rymsdyk
and engraved by Charles Grignion. The 'Ninth Table represents the *uterus* in the eighth or
ninth month of pregnancy.' After several observations on the variable size of the foetus he
recommends the reader to 'consult Dr Hunter's elegant plates of the gravid uterus.'
(see Plates 38 and 39).

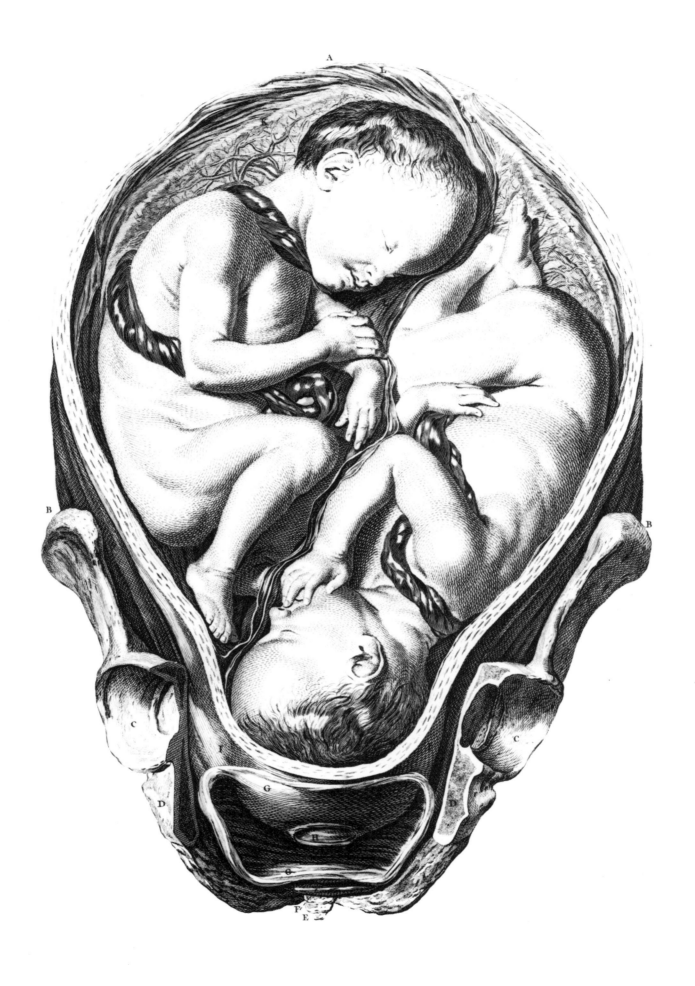

PLATE 37

WILLIAM SMELLIE, *Sett of Anatomical Tables*, 1754, Table X. Drawn by Jan van Rymsdyk
and engraved by Charles Grignion. The 'Tenth Table gives a front view of twins in *utero*, in
the beginning of labour, the anterior parts being removed.'

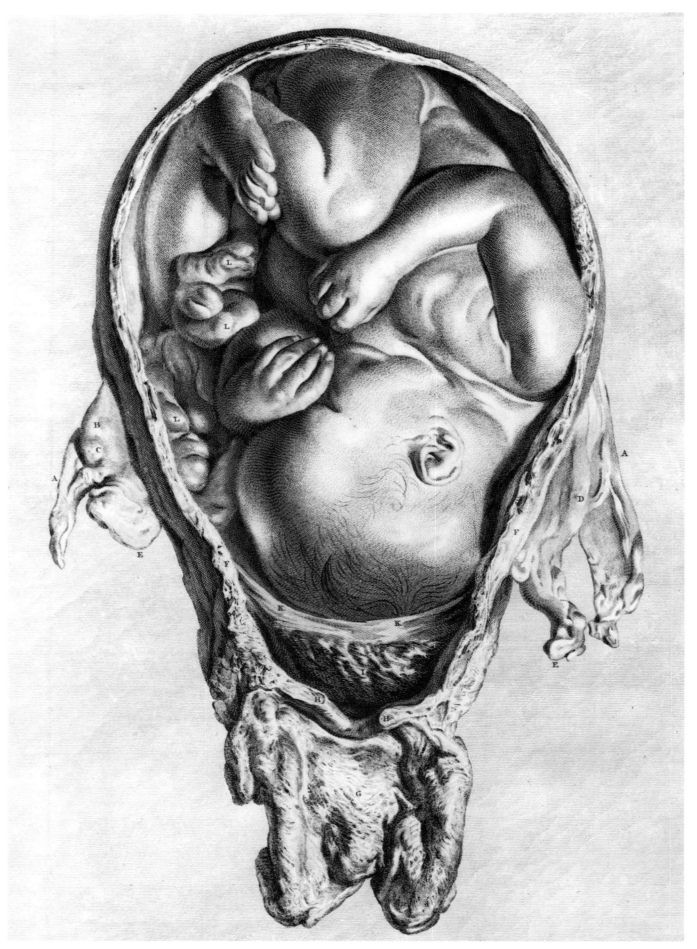

PLATE 38

WILLIAM HUNTER, *Gravid Uterus*, 1774, Table XII. Drawn by Jan van Rymsdyk and engraved by J. Mitchell. 'A view of the womb and vagina fully opened up the back part to show the situation of the child, and of the lower part of the placenta at the inside of the mouth of the womb, under the child's head, and detached from the womb; the occasion of the fatal hemmorhage (sic).'

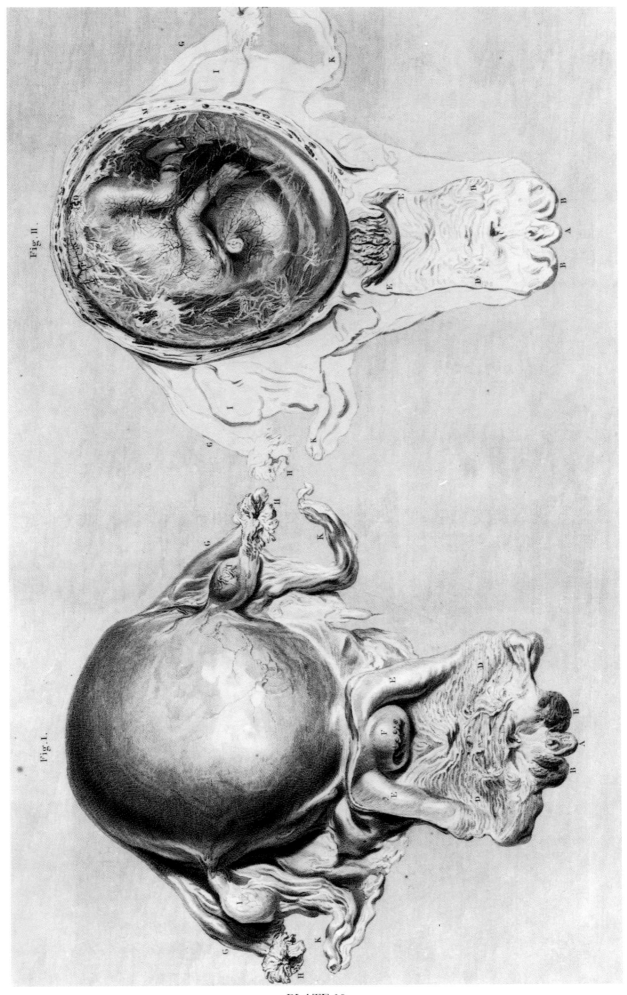

PLATE 39

WILLIAM HUNTER, *Gravid Uterus*, 1774, Table XXVII. Drawn by Jan van Rymsdyk and engraved by Canot. The womb in the fifth month of pregnancy.

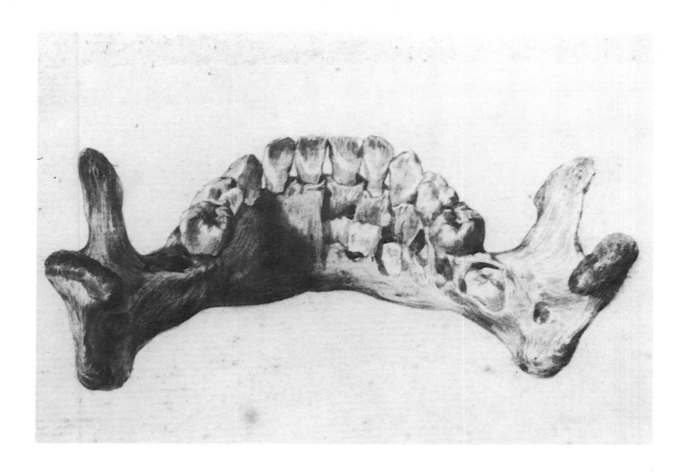

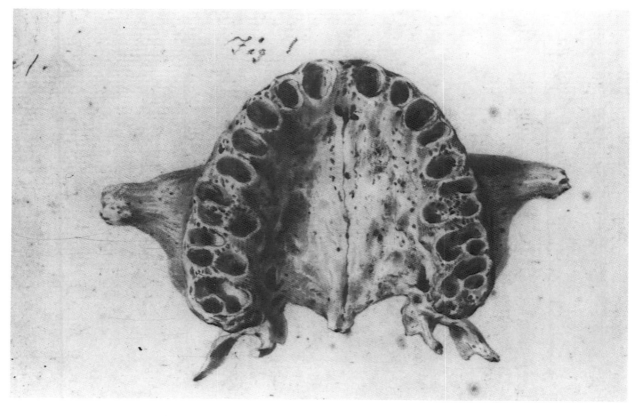

PLATE 40

JAN VAN RYMSDYK, original chalk drawing *c*.1755 of the lower jaw (a) and of the upper jaw
seen from below (b) for John Hunter's *Natural History of the Human Teeth*, 1771.

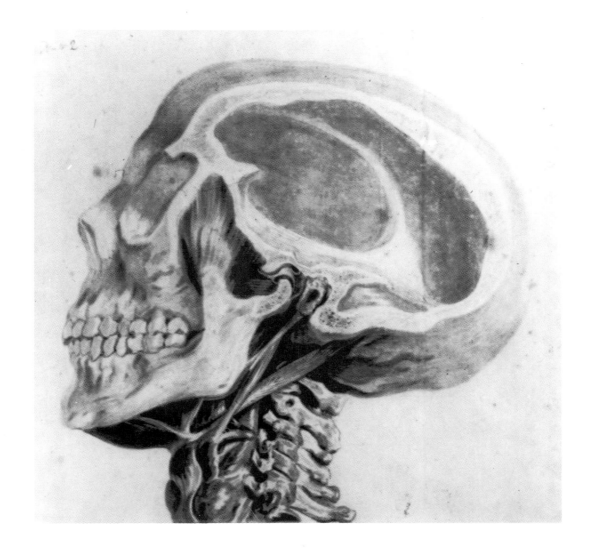

PLATE 41
JAN VAN RYMSDYK, original chalk drawing *c.*1755 of the skull and vertebrae of the neck for
John Hunter's *Natural History of the Human Teeth*, 1771.

THE WORKS OF THE LATE PROFESSOR CAMPER (1794)

by

Petrus Camper

Photographs: British Museum

Camper was a physician, anatomist and naturalist. He had been introduced to drawing when young and he painted, etched and drew in charcoal and pastel. He also worked as a sculptor. Camper believed that anatomical subjects should be drawn like architecture – to scale, with actual measurements, not drawn from observation "in perspective" as had usually been the practice. He became famous through his investigation of the mathematical structure of the human head. He was appointed Professer of Anatomy and Surgery at Amsterdam in 1755.

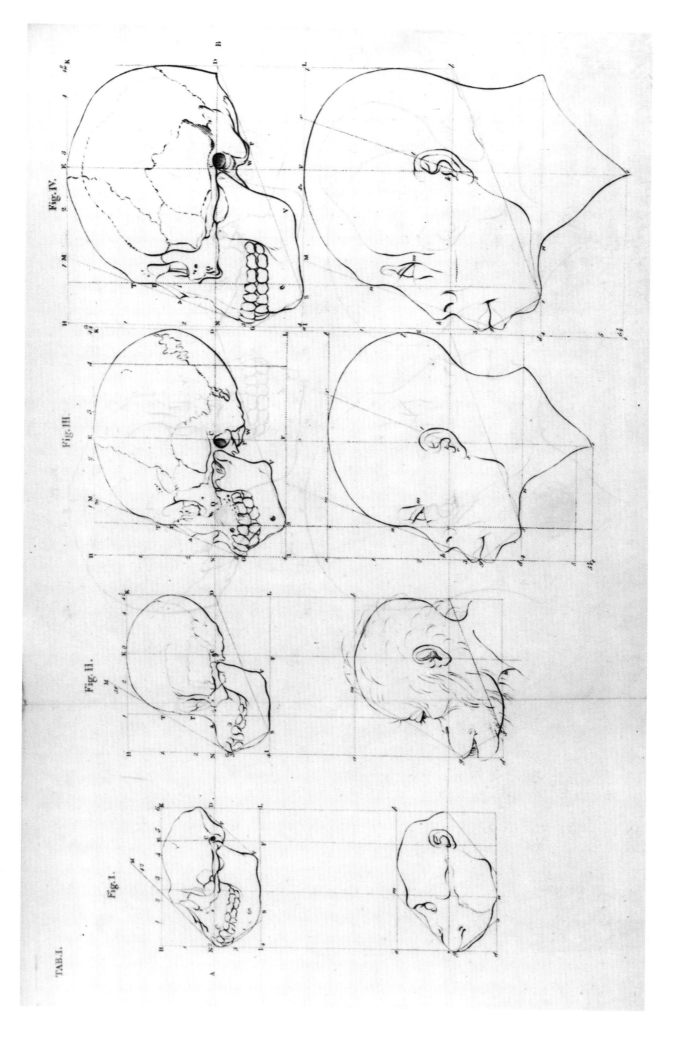

PLATE 42

PETRUS CAMPER, *The Works of the Late Prof. Camper*, 1794, Table I. Camper was
particularly interested in comparative anatomy as can be seen here.

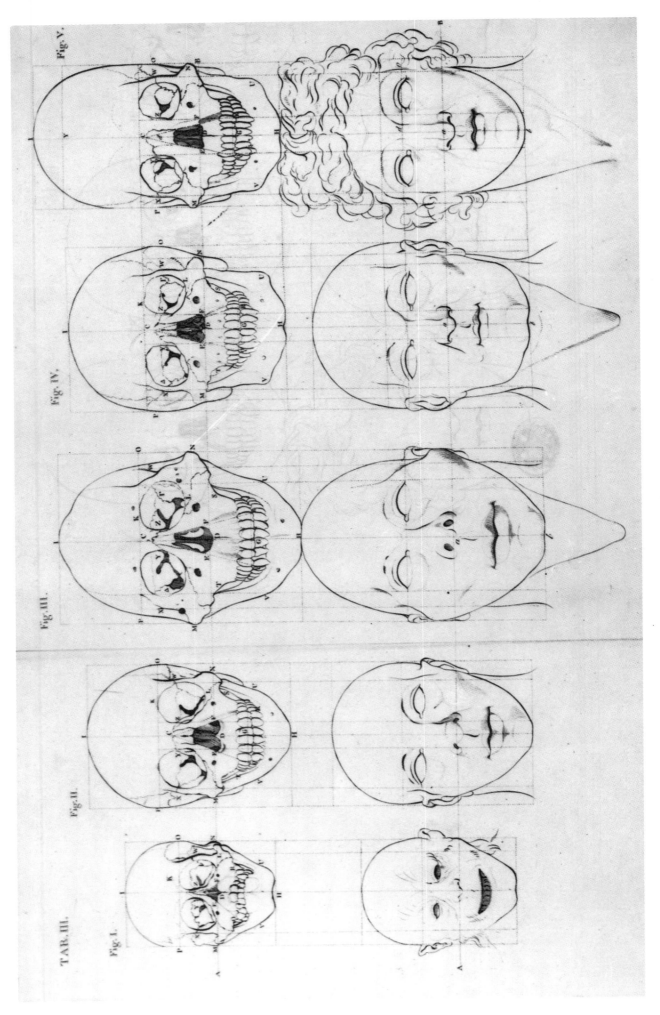

PLATE 43

PETRUS CAMPER, *The Works of the Late Prof. Camper*, 1794, Table III. Apart from exploring the skulls of different races and physical types, Camper also includes an ancient Roman marble head.

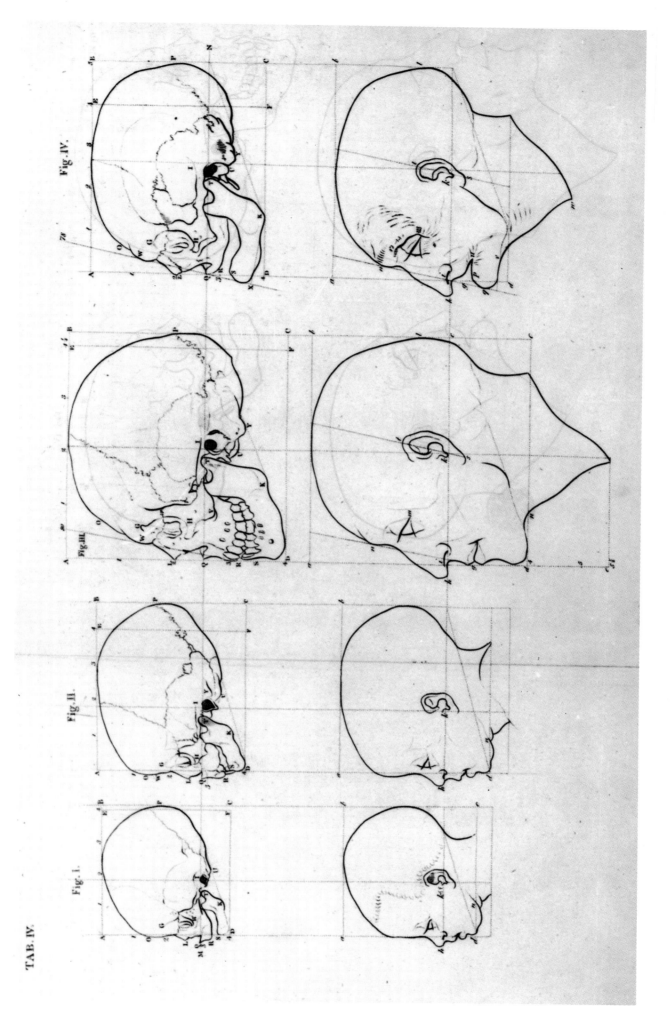

PLATE 44
Petrus Camper, *The Works of the Late Prof. Camper*, 1794, Table IV. Camper here studies
the ages of man, from babyhood to old age.

MUSEUM ANATOMICUM
ACADEMIAE LUGDUNO-BATAVIAE
(1793–1835)

by

Eduard Sandifort

Artist: Abraham Delfos

Engraved by either Robert Muis or Pieter de Mare

Photographs: Bernard Quaritch

Called the 'father of pathological iconography', Eduard Sandifort succeeded Albinus as Professor of Anatomy and Surgery at Leyden University. Like Albinus, Sandifort was concerned with developing the 'perfect' anatomical drawing. His book reflects the collection of the anatomy department of the University, with the first volume containing nine copperplate engravings depicting skulls from different countries around the world.

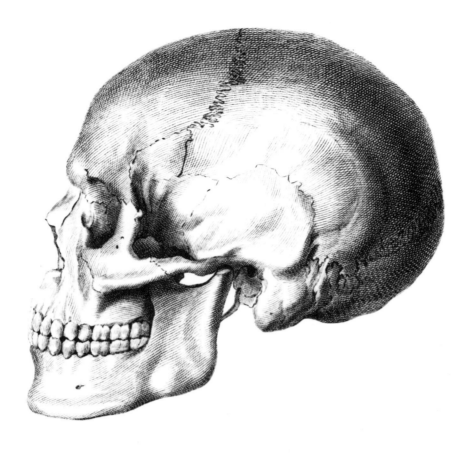

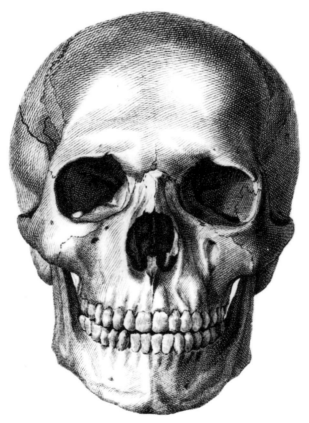

CRANIUM ANGLI.

PLATE 45
EDUARD SANDIFORT, *Museum Anatomicum Academiae Lugduno-Bataviae*, Vol I, 1793–1835.
Drawn by Abraham Delfos and engraved by either Robert Muis or Pieter de Mare. The
skull of an English person.

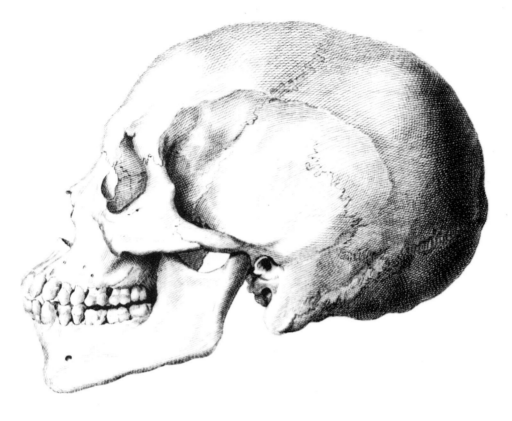

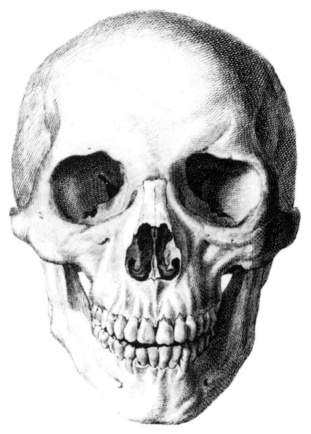

CRANIUM AETHIOPIS.

PLATE 46
EDUARD SANDIFORT, *Museum Anatomicum*, Vol. I, 1793–1835. Drawn by Abraham Delfos
and engraved by either Robert Muis or Pieter de Mare. The skull of an Ethiopian.

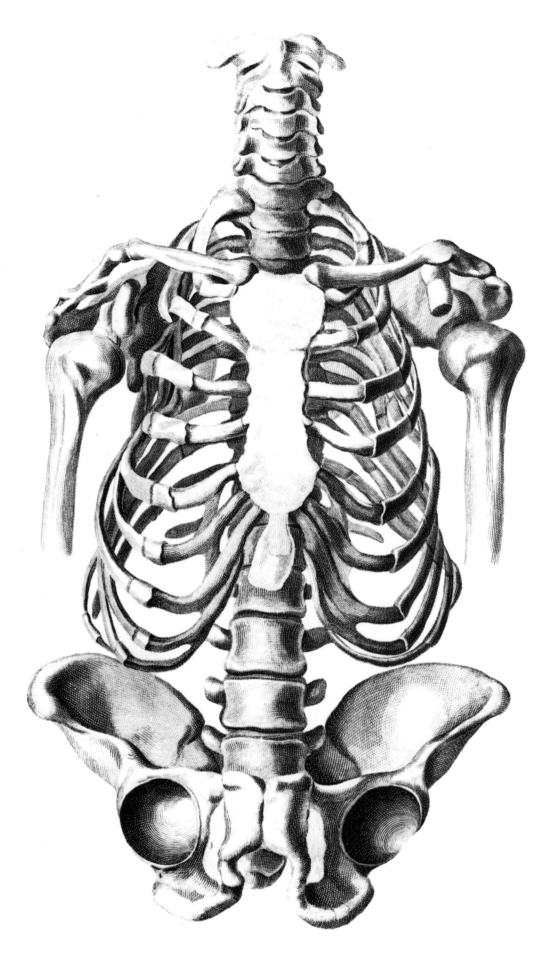

PLATE 47

Eduard Sandifort, *Museum Anatomicum*, Vol. II, 1793–1835, Plate I. Drawn by
Abraham Delfos and engraved by either Robert Muis or Pieter de Mare. Truncated female
skeleton seen from the front. This drawing was obviously made from a specific skeleton since
it shows marked distortions in the ribs and pelvis.

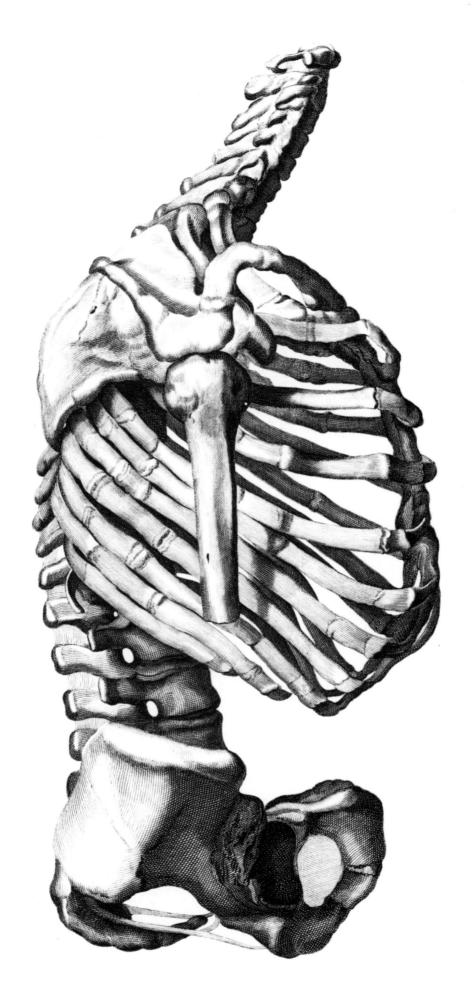

PLATE 48
EDUARD SANDIFORT, *Museum Anatomicum*, Vol. II, 1793–1835, Plate II. Drawn by
Abraham Delfos and engraved by either Robert Muis or Pieter de Mare. The side view of the
female skeleton seen in Plate 47.

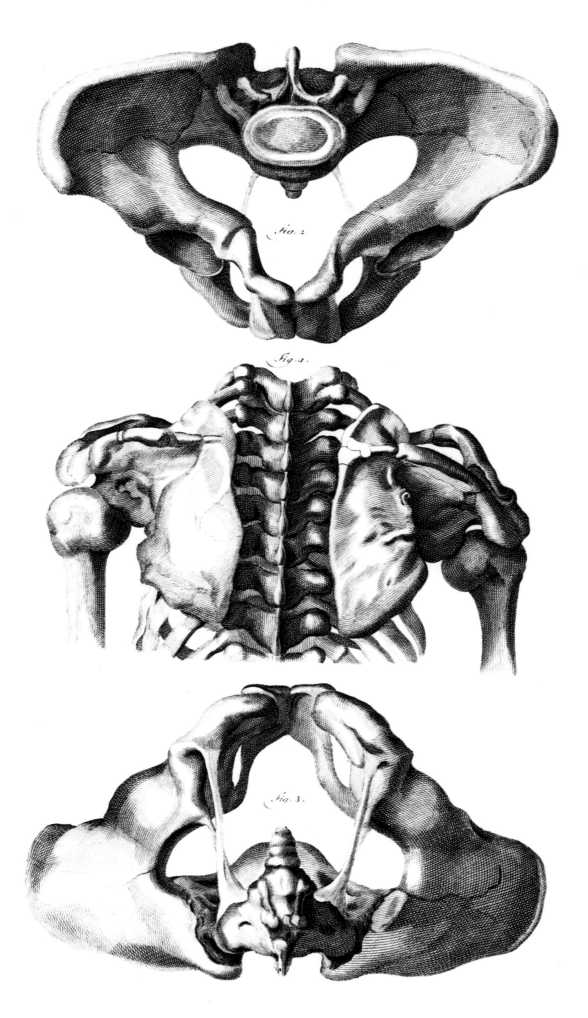

PLATE 49

EDUARD SANDIFORT, *Museum Anatomicum*, Vol. II, 1793–1835, Plate IIII. Drawn by
Abraham Delfos and engraved by either Robert Muis or Pieter de Mare. The central
illustration shows a back view of the bones of the shoulders and upper torso, and above and
below it are views of a pelvis.

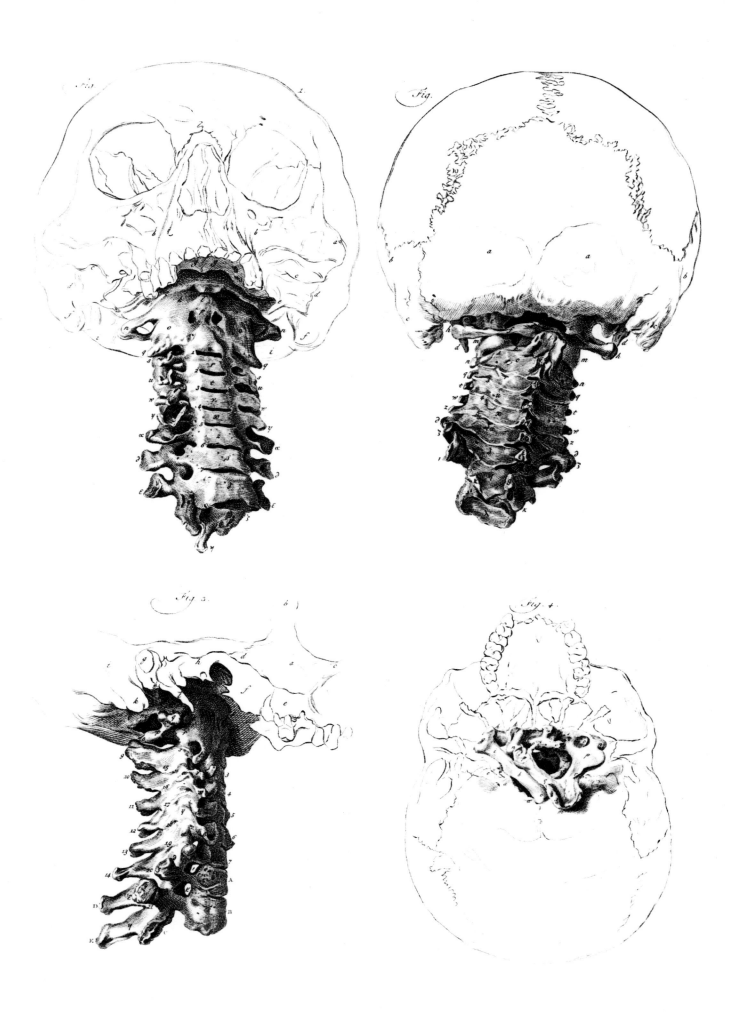

PLATE 50
EDUARD SANDIFORT, *Museum Anatomicum*, Vol. II, 1793–1835, Plate XV. Drawn by
Abraham Delfos and engraved either by Robert Muis or Pieter de Mare. Studies of the
vertebrae of the neck in relation to the skull.

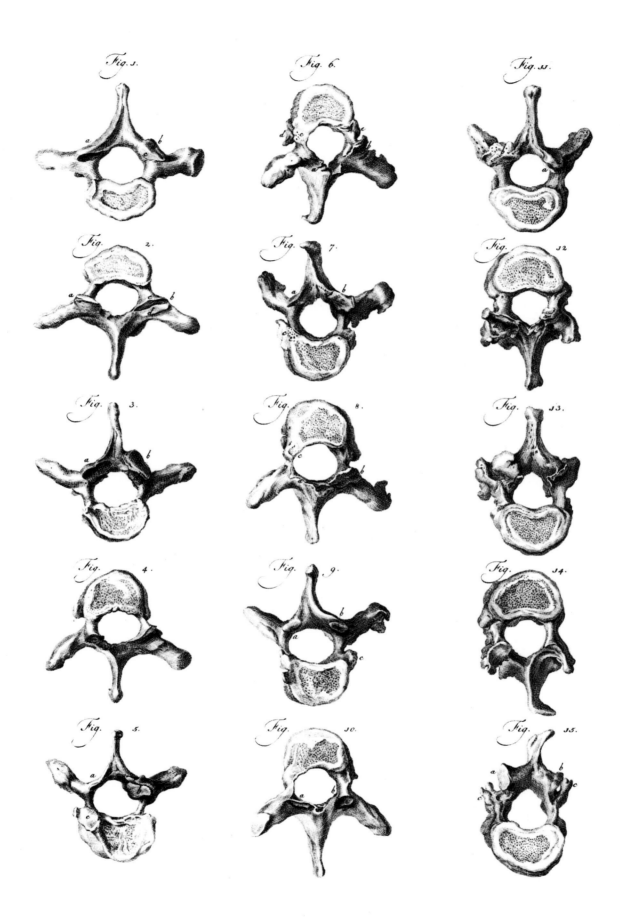

PLATE 51

EDUARD SANDIFORT, *Museum Anatomicum*, Vol. II, 1793–1835, Plate XXXVI. Drawn by
Abraham Delfos and engraved either by Robert Muis or Pieter de Mare. Studies of vertebrae
from a male skeleton showing the effects of manual labour and of degenerative disease.

ANATOMIA PER USO DEI PITTORI E SCULTORI (1811)

by

Giuseppe del Medico

Photographs: Bernard Quaritch

Little is known of del Medico's life or career. This book was introduced at the Academy of Arts in Rome as a manual of anatomy for artists. In style, del Medico's book anticipates later anatomical works, for although there are references to fine art and to earlier neo-classical traditions (for example, the depiction of the famous Borghese gladiator in plates 65 and 66), the emphasis is more on clarity and layout than on decorative qualities.

The complete skeletons in Plates 52, 53 and 64 are said to be after Albinus (see plates 26–32).

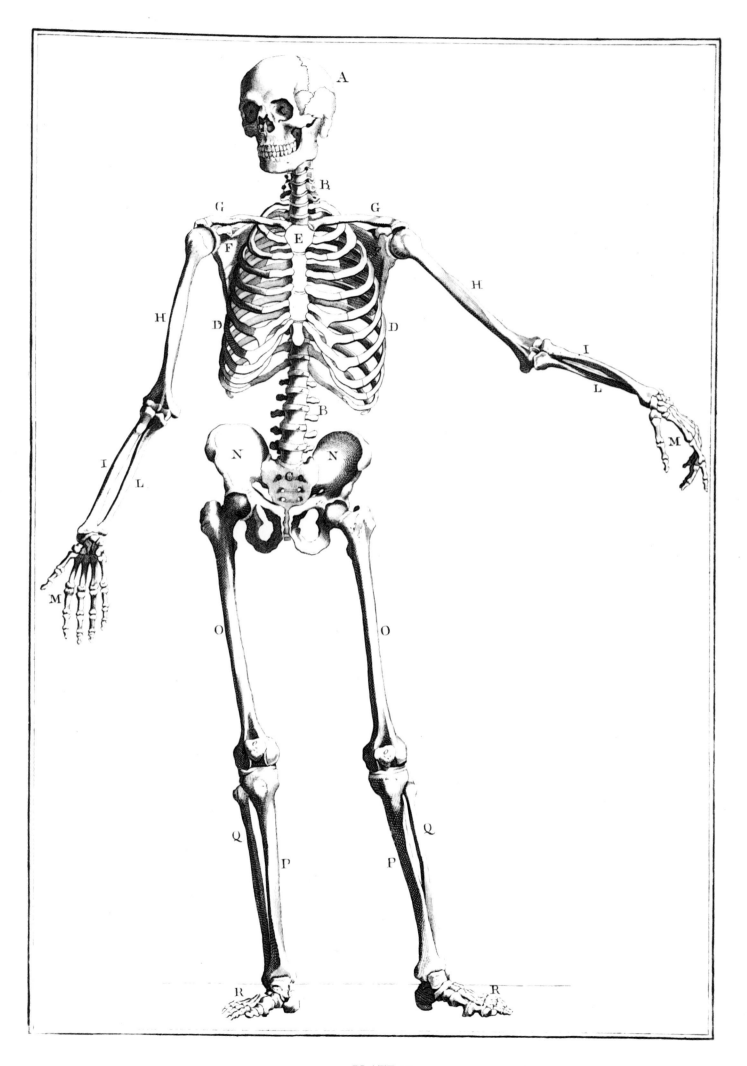

PLATE 52

GIUSEPPE DEL MEDICO, *Anatomia per Uso dei Pittori e Scultori*, 1811, Tavola 1. Possibly drawn
and engraved by Del Medico himself. Figure outlining the different parts of the skeleton.

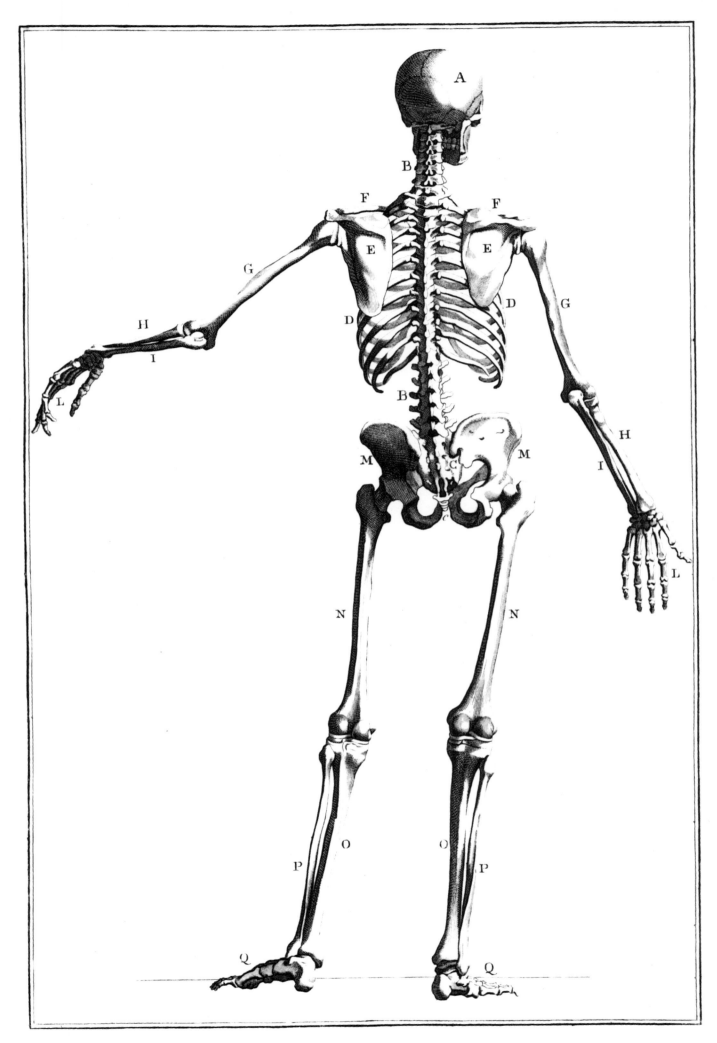

PLATE 53

GIUSEPPE DEL MEDICO, *Anatomia per Uso dei Pittori e Scultori*, 1811, Tavola 2. The same
skeleton as in Plate 52 but seen from the back.

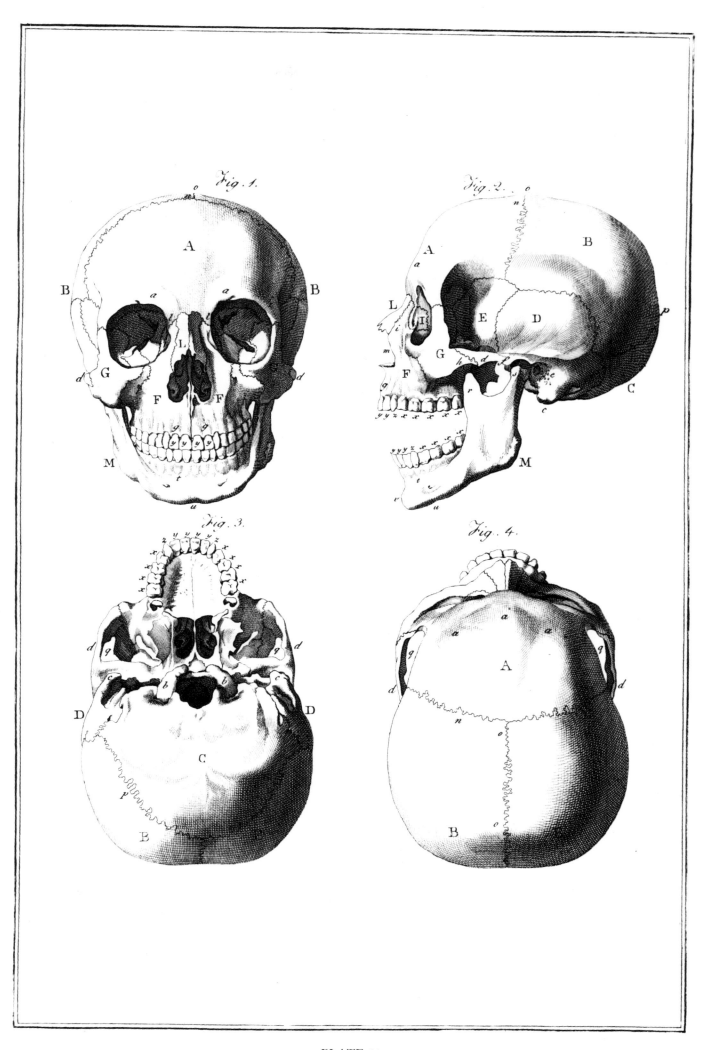

PLATE 54
GIUSEPPE DEL MEDICO, *Anatomia per Uso dei Pittori e Scultori*, 1811, Tavola 3. Four views
of the skull.

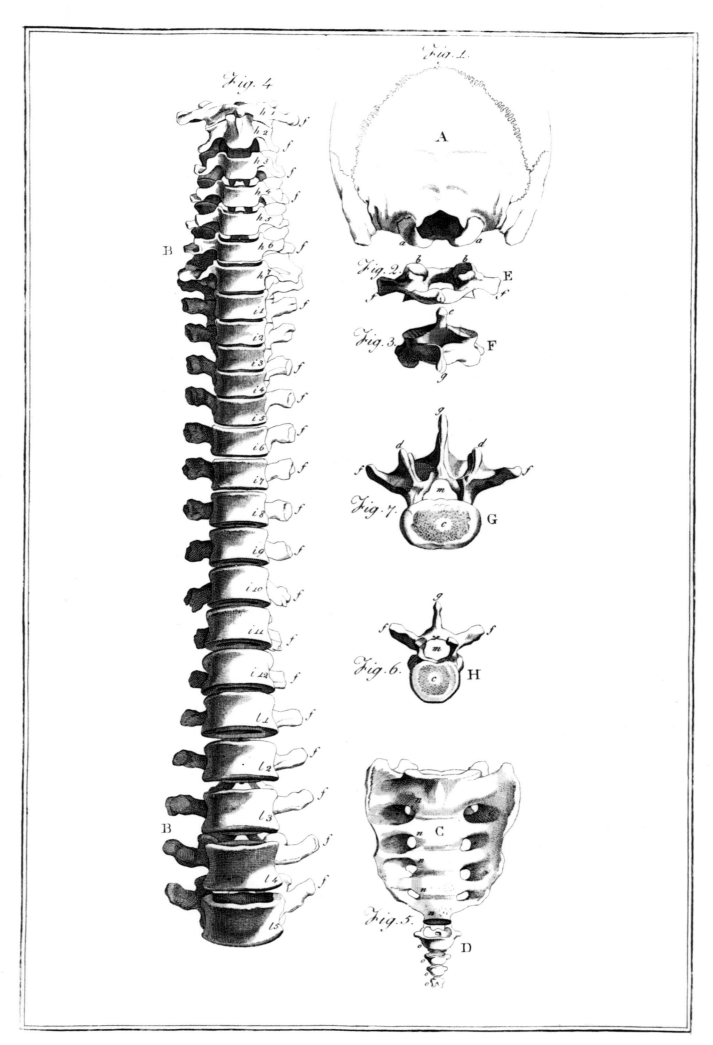

PLATE 55
GIUSEPPE DEL MEDICO, *Anatomia per Uso dei Pittori e Scultori*, 1811, Tavola 4. Studies of
the spine and of individual vertebrae.

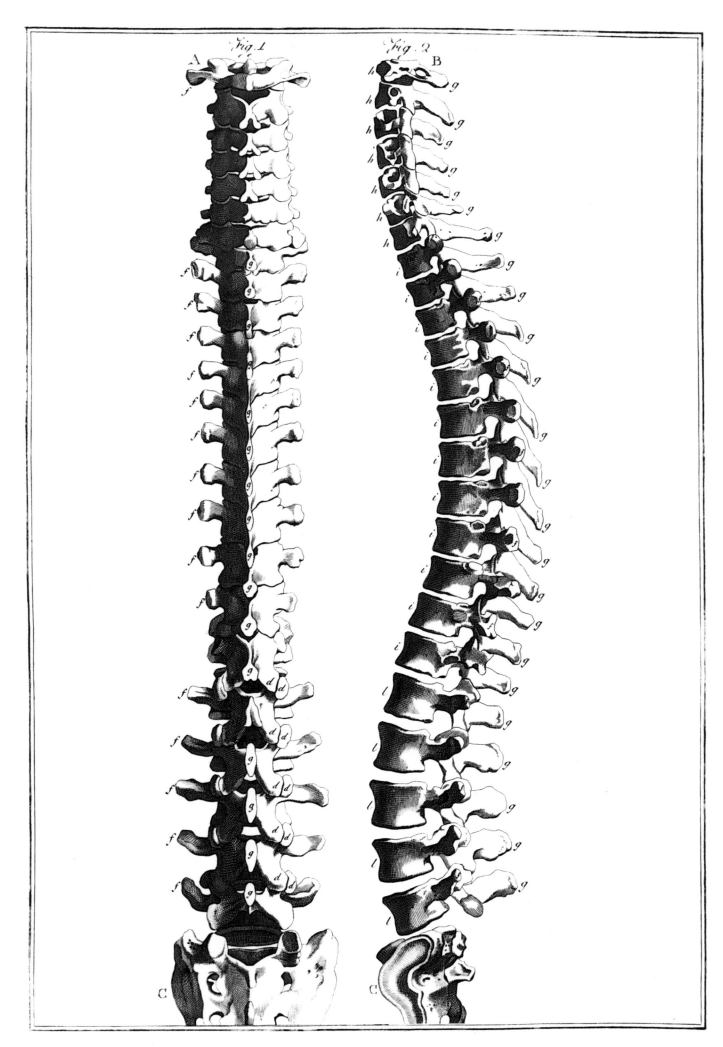

PLATE 56

GIUSEPPE DEL MEDICO, *Anatomia per Uso dei Pittori e Scultori*, 1811, Tavola 5. Studies of
the spine.

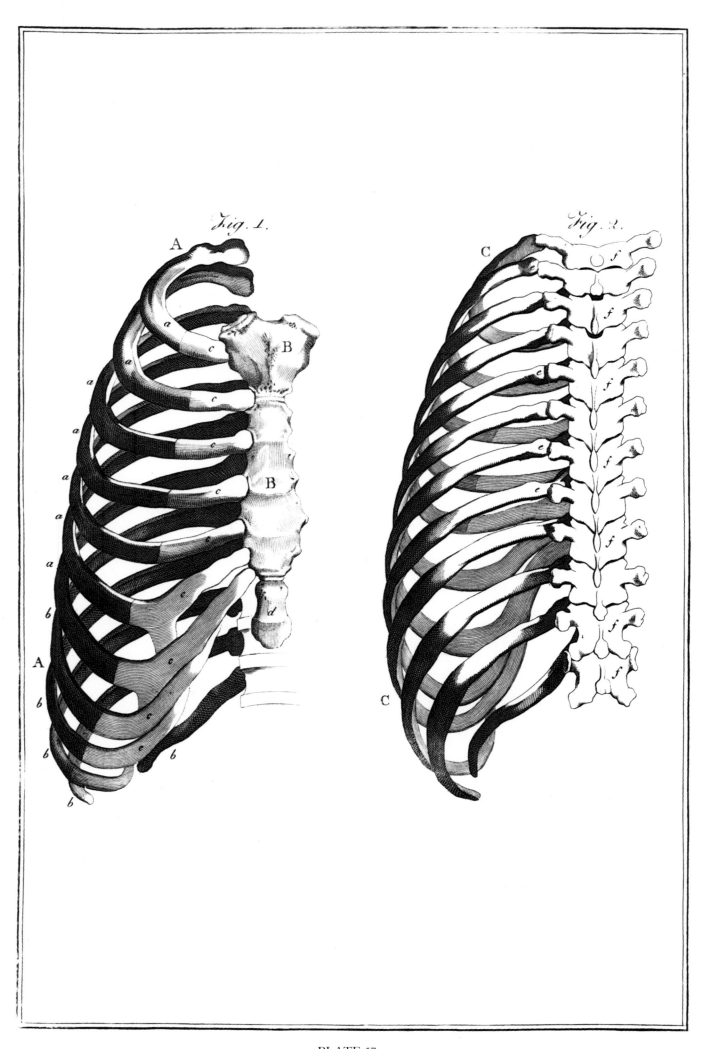

PLATE 57

GIUSEPPE DEL MEDICO, *Anatomia per Uso dei Pittori e Scultori*, 1811, Tavola 6. Studies of
the rib cage from front and back.

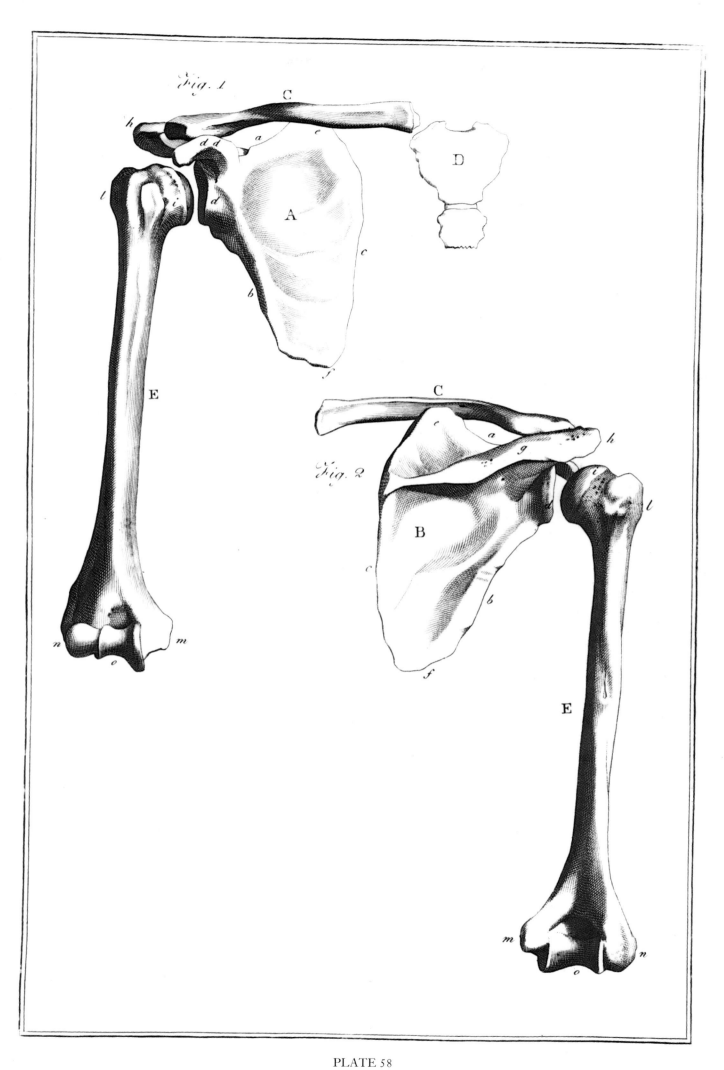

PLATE 58
GIUSEPPE DEL MEDICO, *Anatomia per Uso dei Pittori e Scultori*, 1811, Tavola 7. The upper
arm, collarbone and shoulder blade seen from front and back.

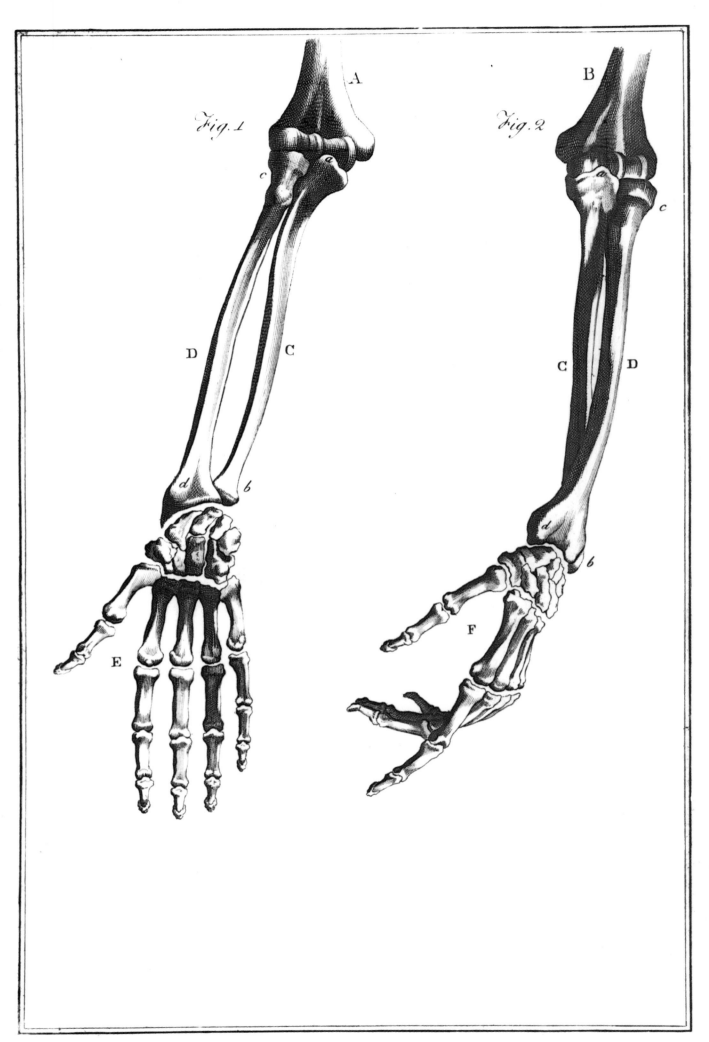

PLATE 59
GIUSEPPE DEL MEDICO, *Anatomia per Uso dei Pittori e Scultori*, 1811, Tavola 8. The
forearm and hand, seen from the front and outer side.

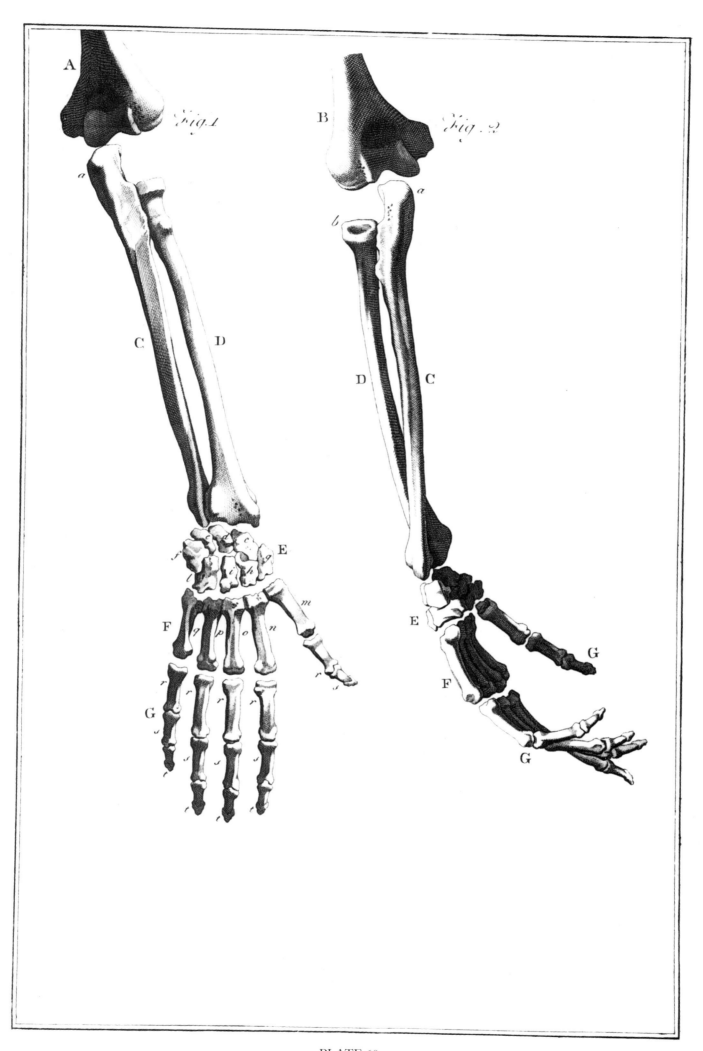

PLATE 60
Giuseppe del Medico, *Anatomia per Uso dei Pittori e Scultori*, 1811, Tavola 9. The
forearm and hand, seen from the back and outer side.

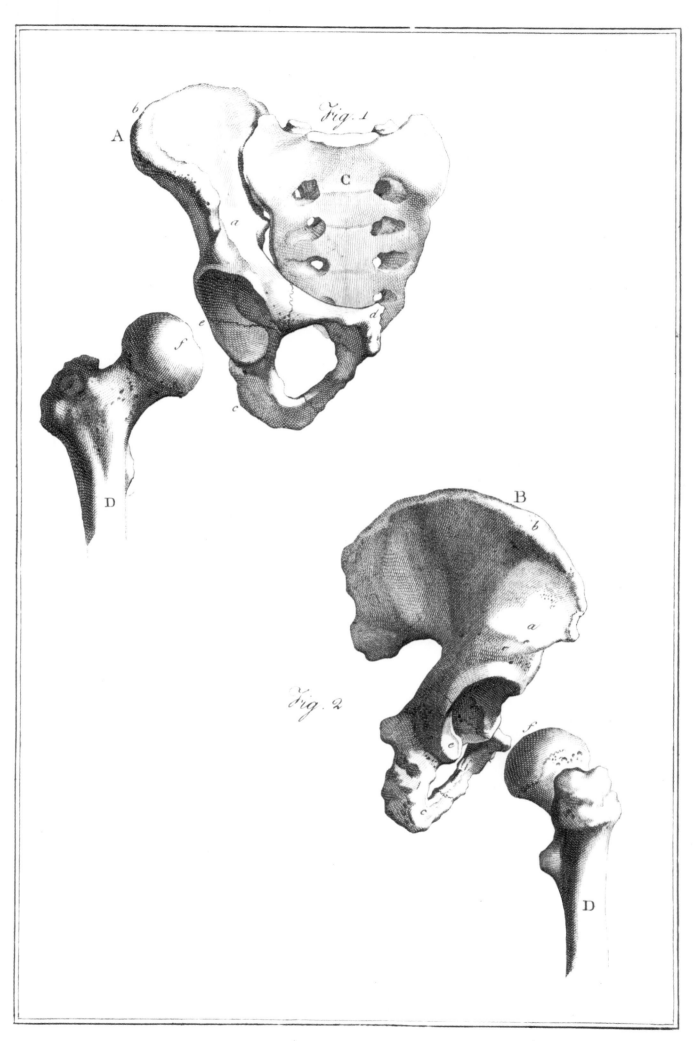

PLATE 61

Giuseppe del Medico, *Anatomia per Uso dei Pittori e Scultori*, 1811, Tavola 10. The hip
joints and pelvis.

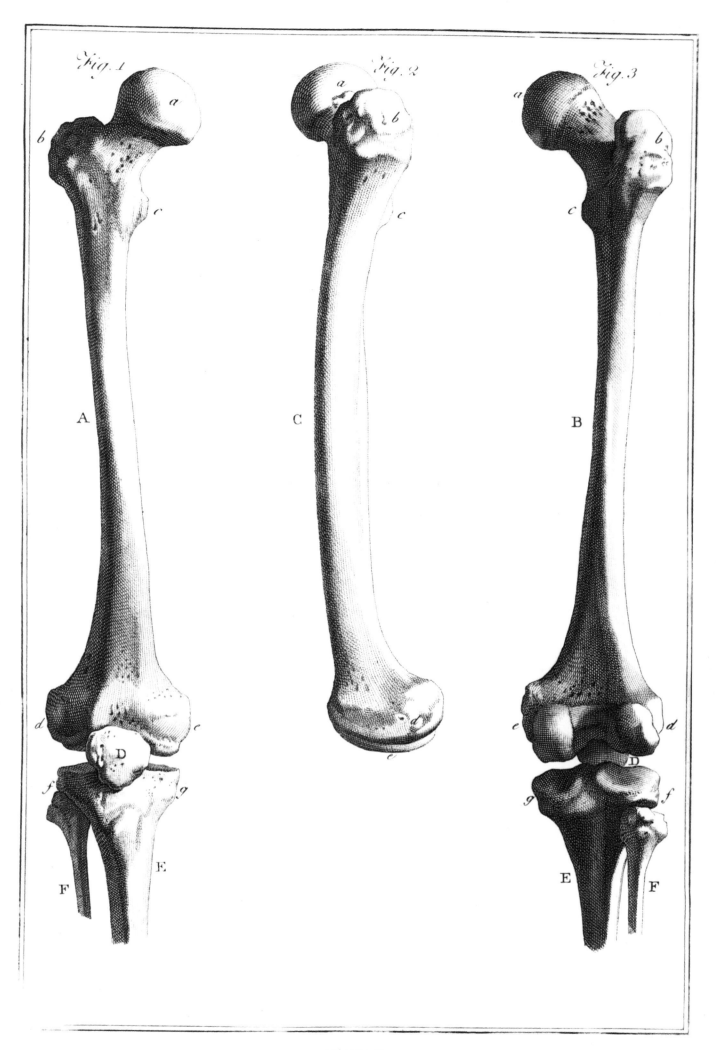

PLATE 62
GIUSEPPE DEL MEDICO, *Anatomia per Uso dei Pittori e Scultori*, 1811, Tavola 11. The femur
and knee joint seen from front and back.

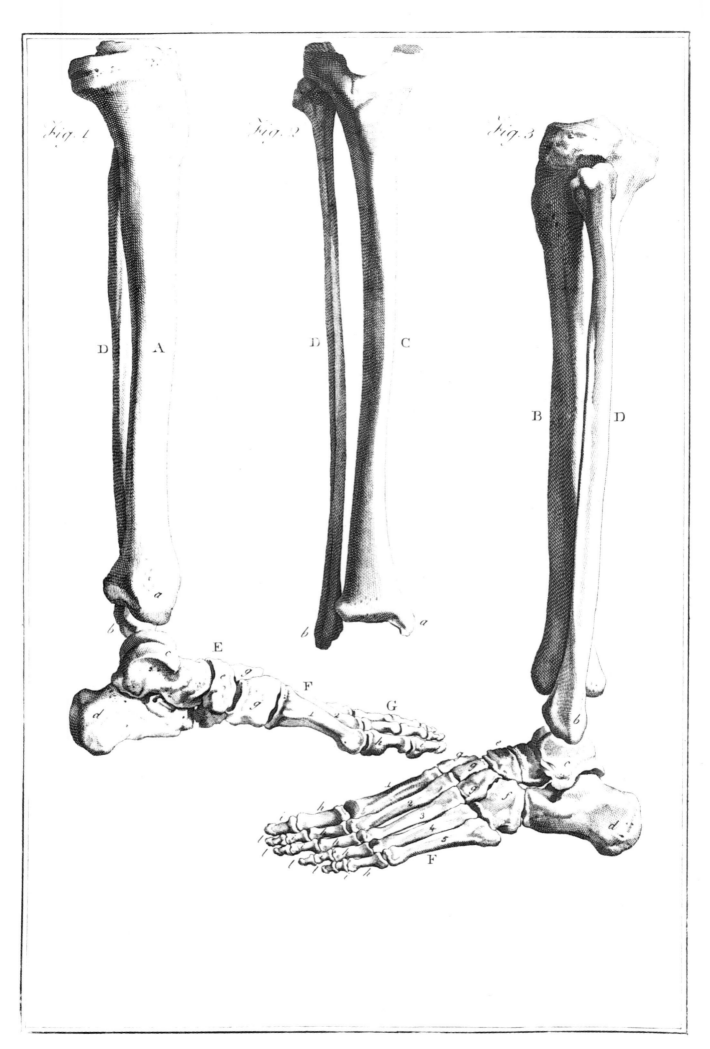

PLATE 63

Giuseppe del Medico, *Anatomia per Uso dei Pittori e Scultori*, 1811, Tavola 12. The bones
of the lower leg, the tibia and the fibula, and those of the foot are depicted from the inner side
and the outer side.

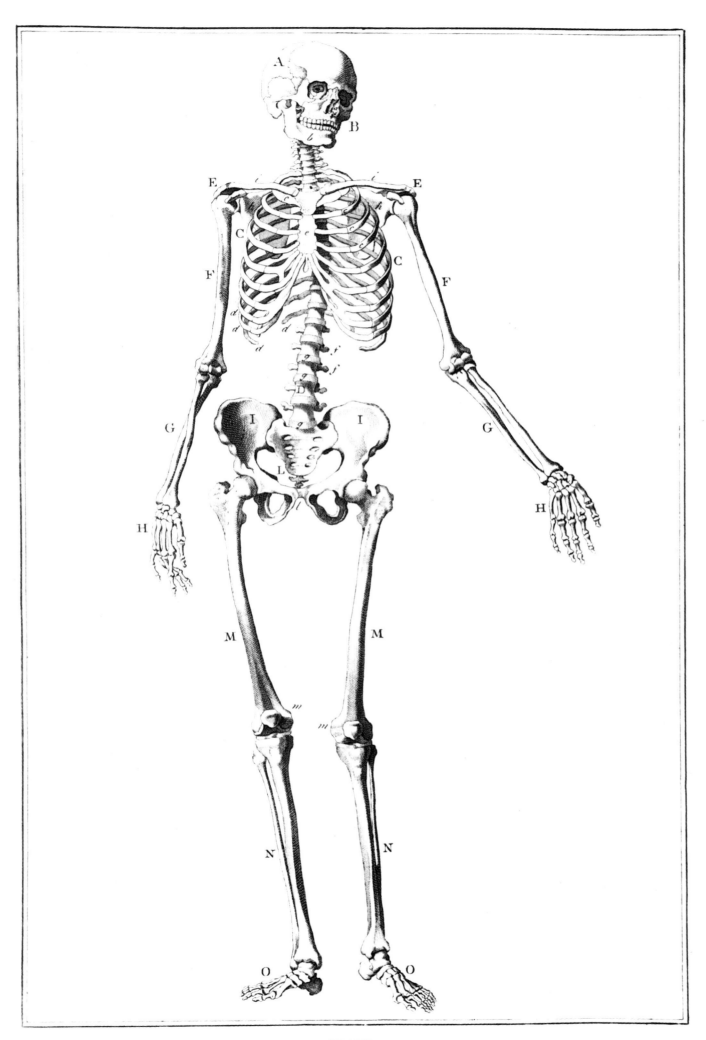

PLATE 64
GIUSEPPE DEL MEDICO, *Anatomia per Uso dei Pittori e Scultori*, 1811, Tavola 13. Standing
skeleton, seen from the front, which is the key to the series of plates depicting the muscles of
the body which follow it, like the skeleton in Plate 52.

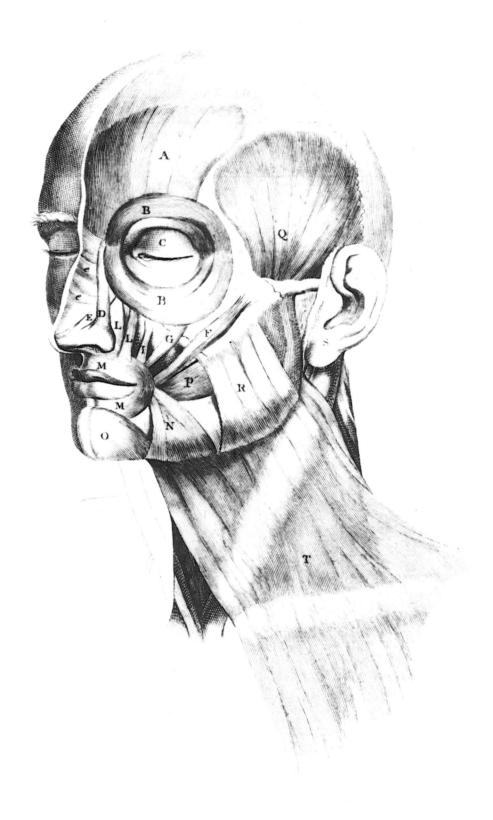

PLATE 65
GIUSEPPE DEL MEDICO, *Anatomia per Uso dei Pittori e Scultori*, 1811, Tavola 14. The
muscles of the head and neck. This image is derived directly from Eustachio.

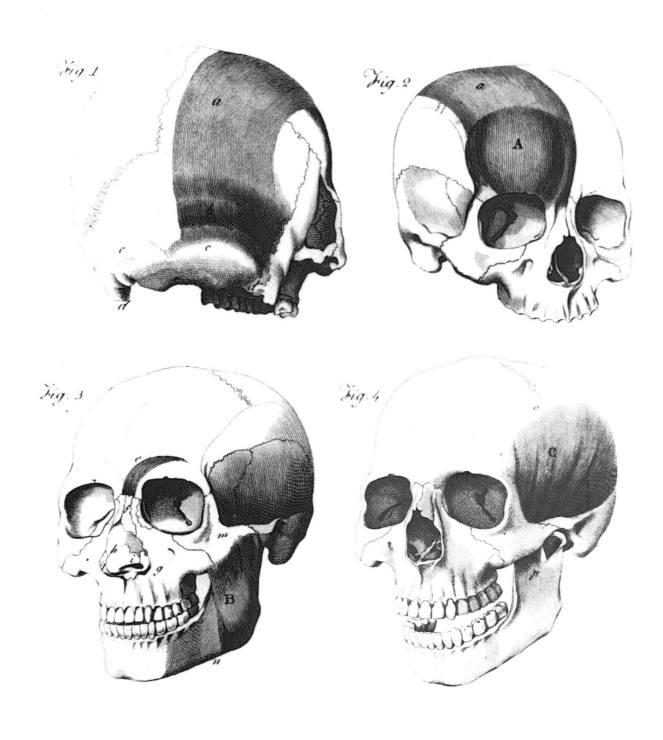

PLATE 66
GIUSEPPE DEL MEDICO, *Anatomia per Uso dei Pittori e Scultori*, 1811, Tavola 15. Four
views of the skull.

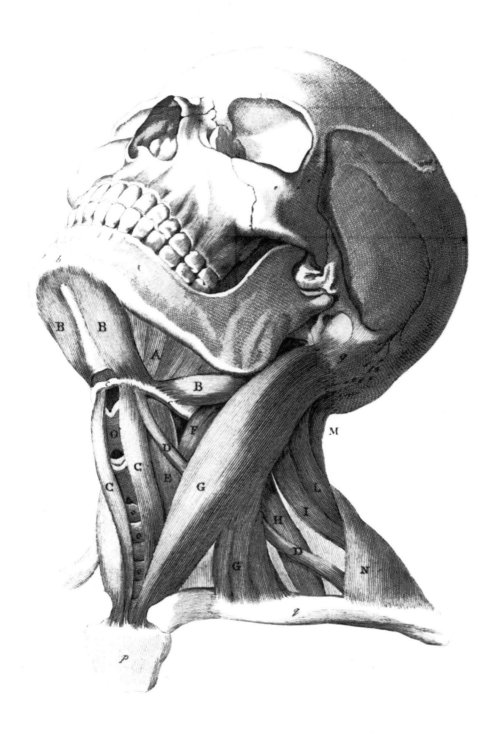

PLATE 67

Giuseppe del Medico, *Anatomia per Uso dei Pittori e Scultori*, 1811, Tavola 16. The muscles of the neck as related to the skull.

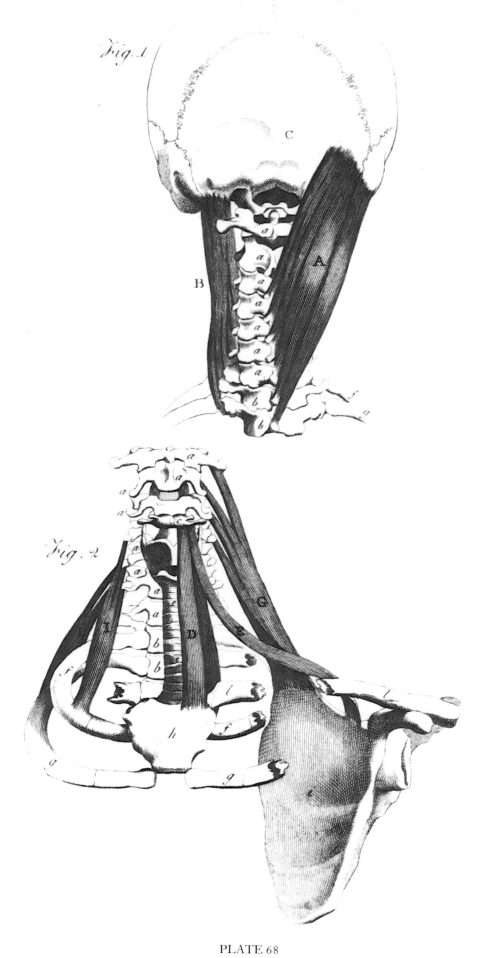

PLATE 68

GIUSEPPE DEL MEDICO, *Anatomia per Uso dei Pittori e Scultori*. 1811, Tavola 17. Two
diagrams demonstrating how the muscles of the neck relate to the back of the skull and to the
ribs and shoulder blade.

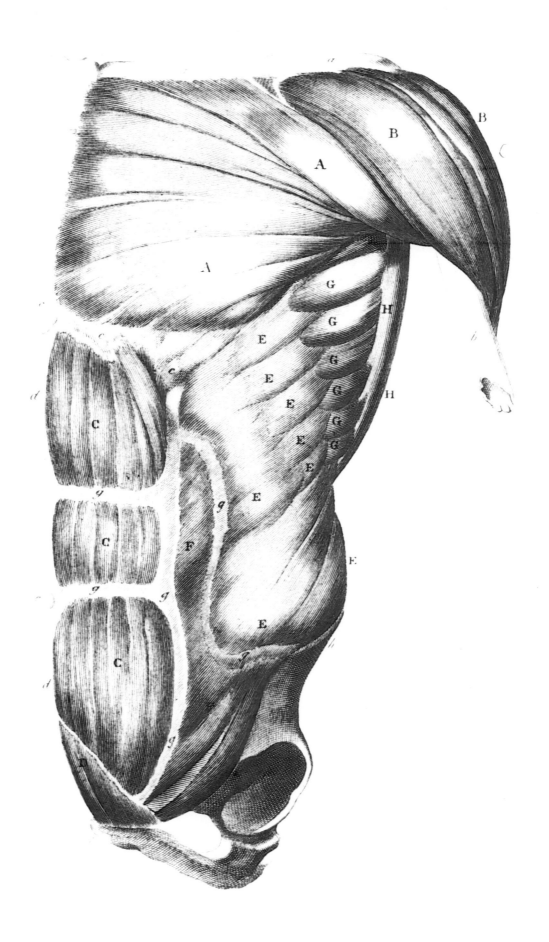

PLATE 69

GIUSEPPE DEL MEDICO, *Anatomia per Uso dei Pittori e Scultori*, 1811, Tavola 18. The
muscles of the torso, front view.

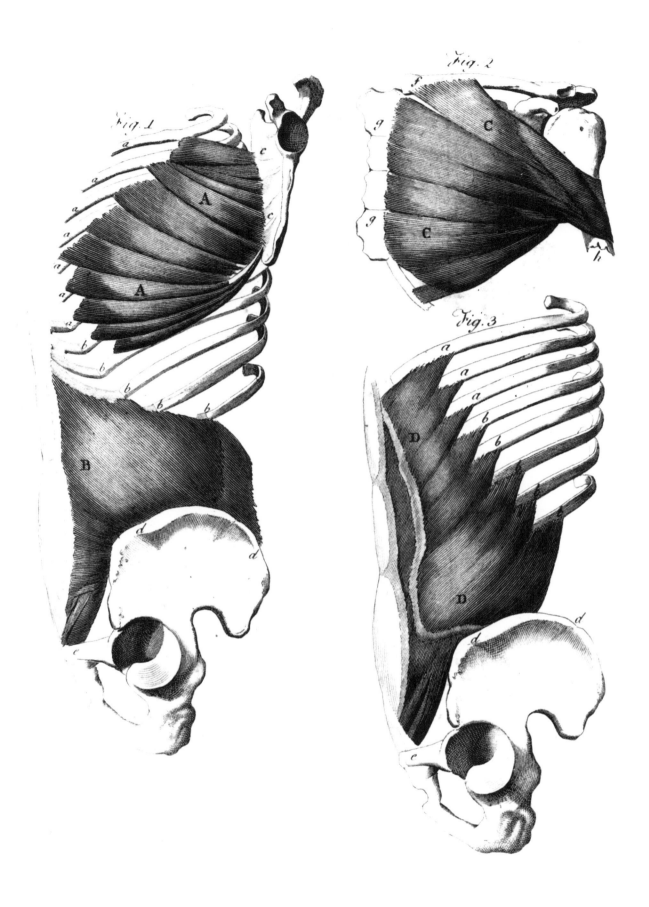

PLATE 70

Giuseppe del Medico, *Anatomia per Uso dei Pittori e Scultori*, 1811, Tavola 19. The
muscles of the torso, side view.

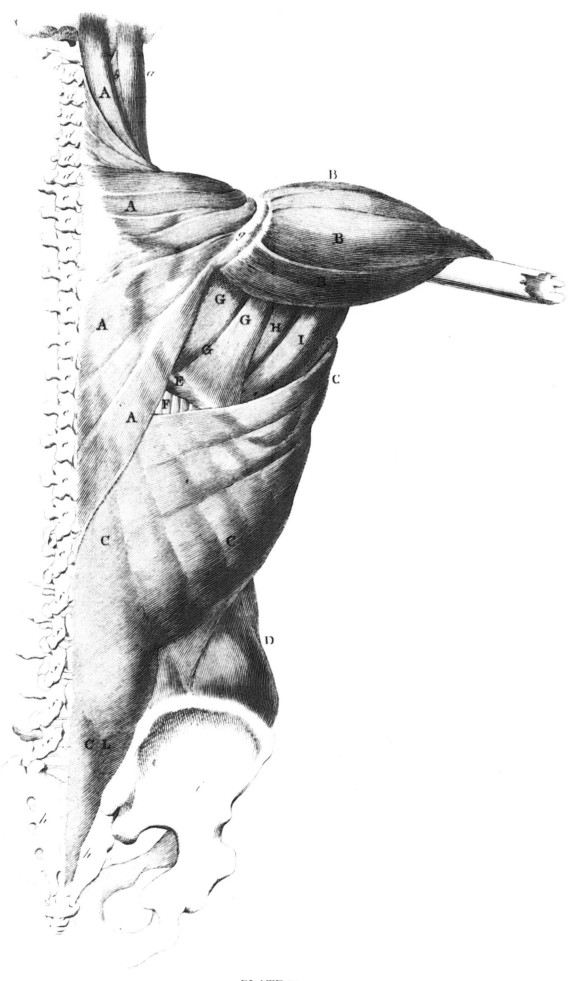

PLATE 71

GIUSEPPE DEL MEDICO, *Anatomia per Uso dei Pittori e Scultori*, 1811, Tavola 20. The
muscles of the torso, back view.

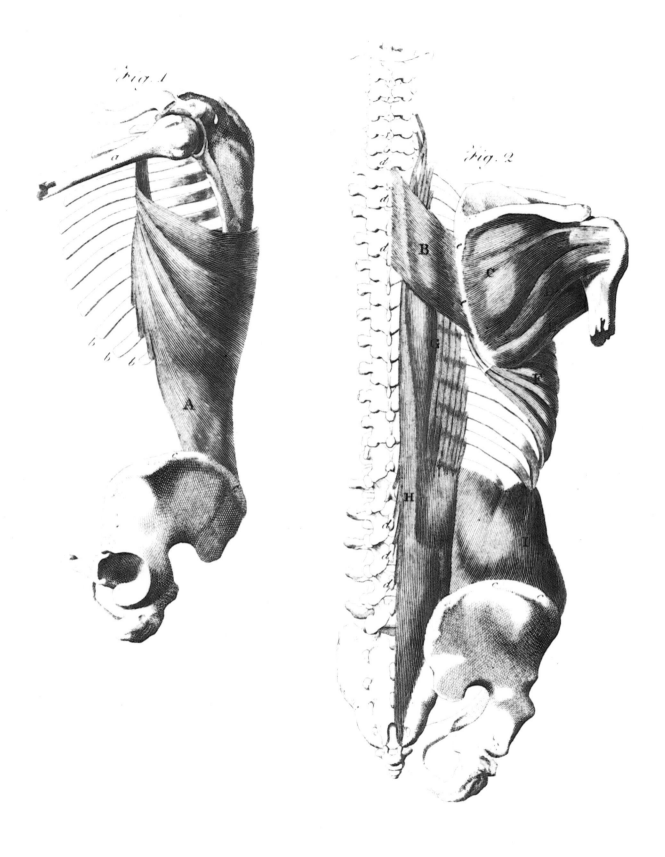

PLATE 72

GIUSEPPE DEL MEDICO, *Anatomia per Uso dei Pittori e Scultori*, 1811, Tavola 21. The
muscles of the torso, back and side view.

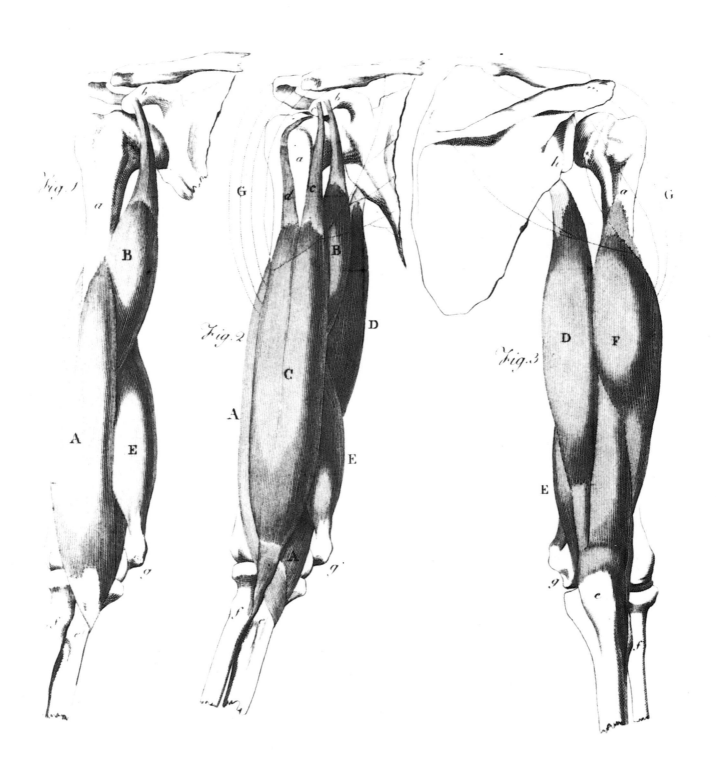

PLATE 73

Giuseppe del Medico, *Anatomia per Uso dei Pittori e Scultori*, 1811, Tavola 22. The muscles of the upper arm.

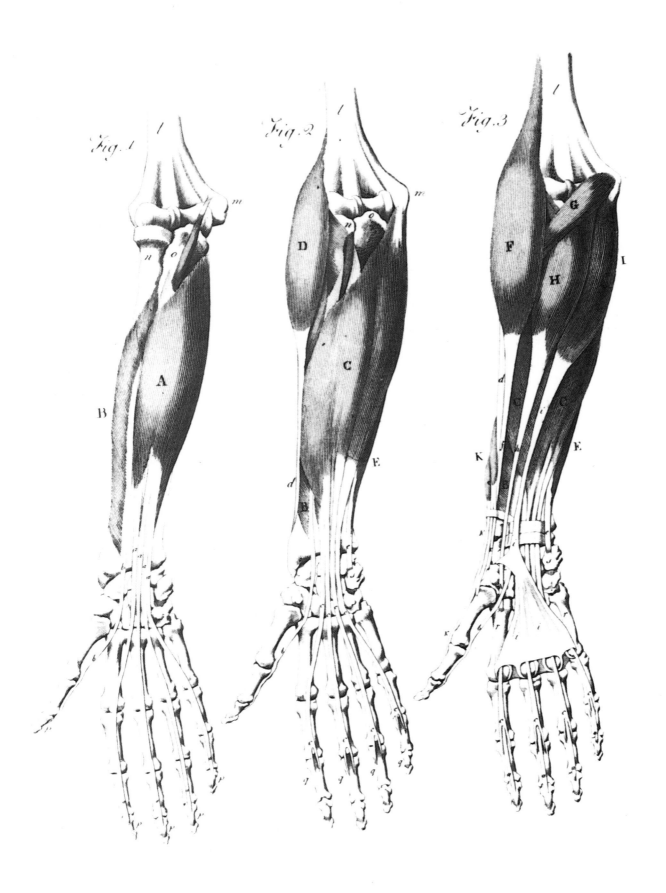

PLATE 74

Giuseppe del Medico, *Anatomia per Uso dei Pittori e Scultori*, 1811, Tavola 23. The muscles of the forearm seen from the side, front and back.

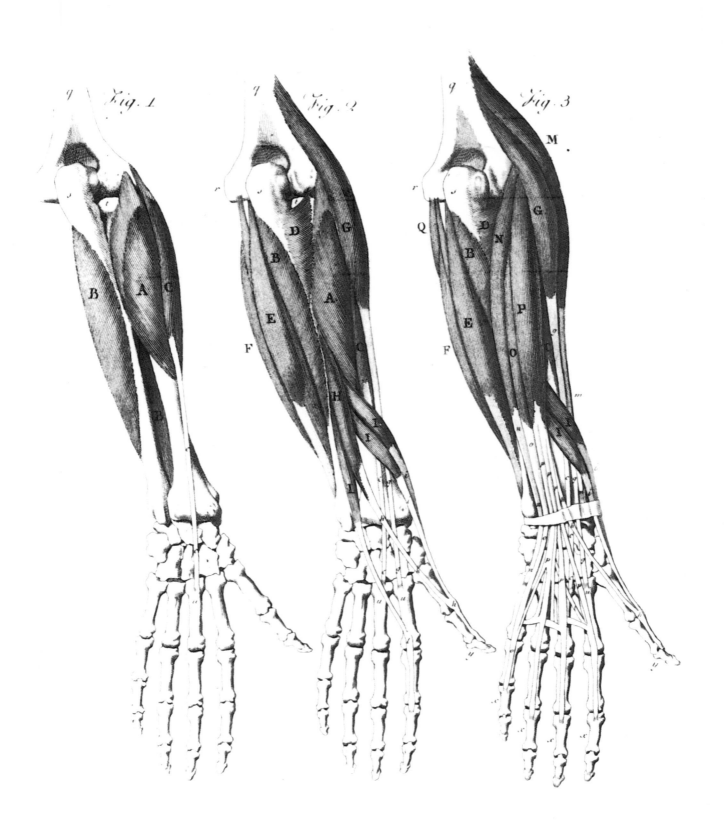

PLATE 75
GIUSEPPE DEL MEDICO, *Anatomia per Uso dei Pittori e Scultori*, 1811, Tavola 24. The muscles of the forearm.

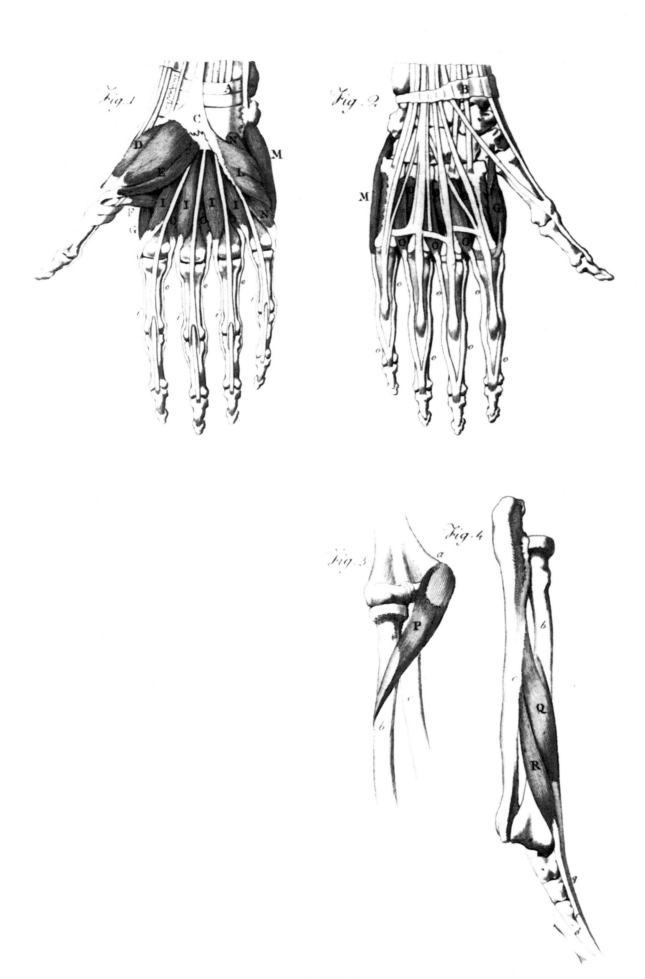

PLATE 76
Giuseppe del Medico, *Anatomia per Uso dei Pittori e Scultori*, 1811, Tavola 25. The
muscles of the hand and elbow.

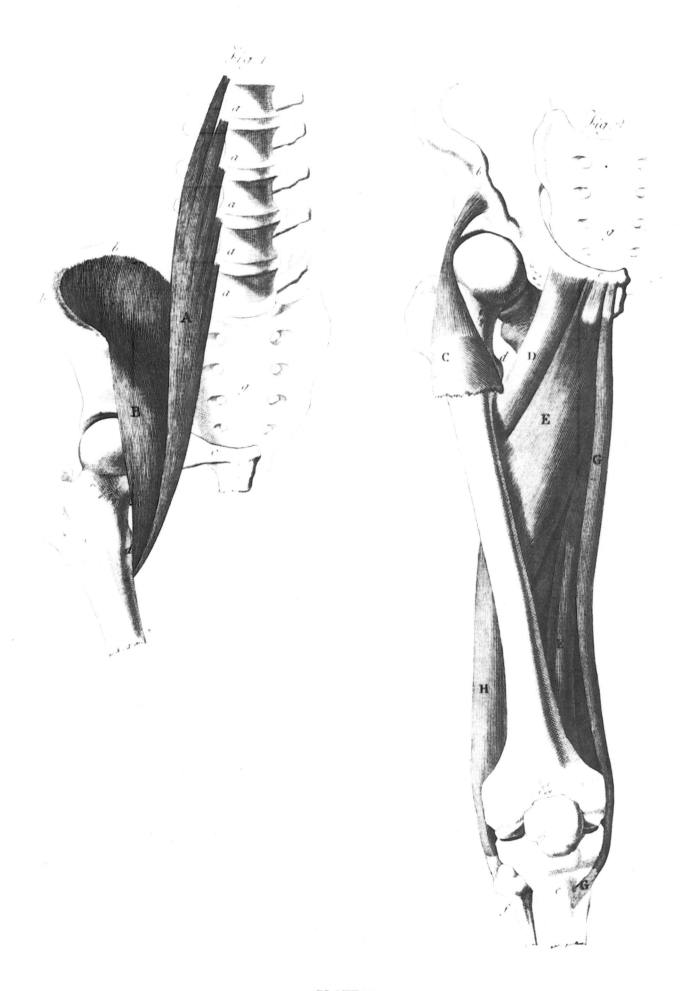

PLATE 77
GIUSEPPE DEL MEDICO, *Anatomia per Uso dei Pittori e Scultori*, 1811, Tavola 27. The
muscles of the hip and thigh.

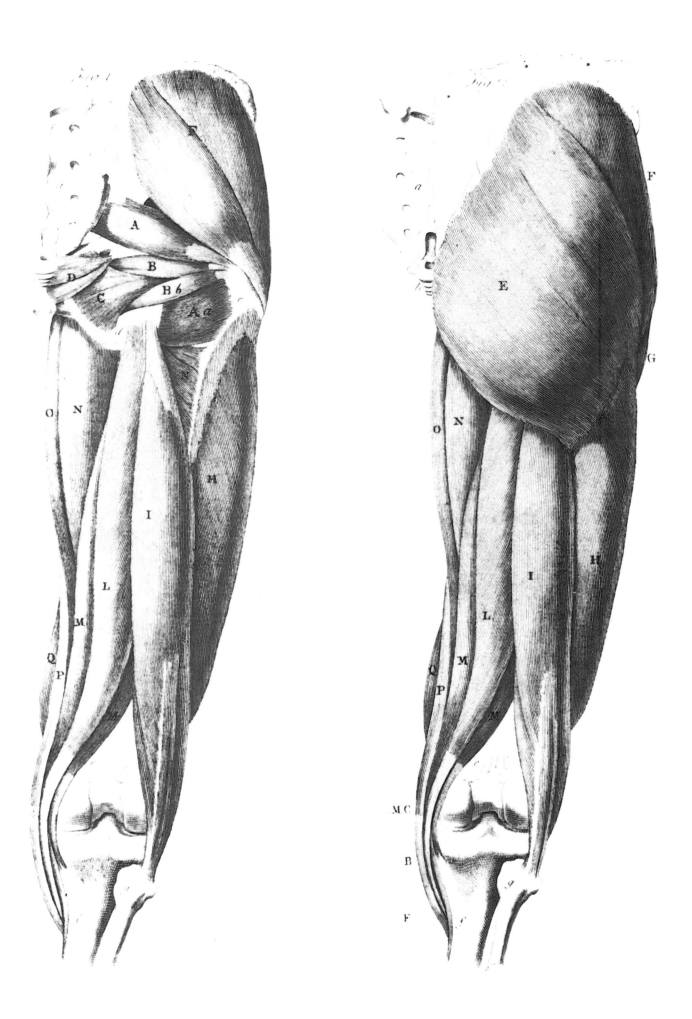

PLATE 78
GIUSEPPE DEL MEDICO, *Anatomia per Uso dei Pittori e Scultori*, 1811, Tavola 28. The
muscles of the upper leg seen from the back.

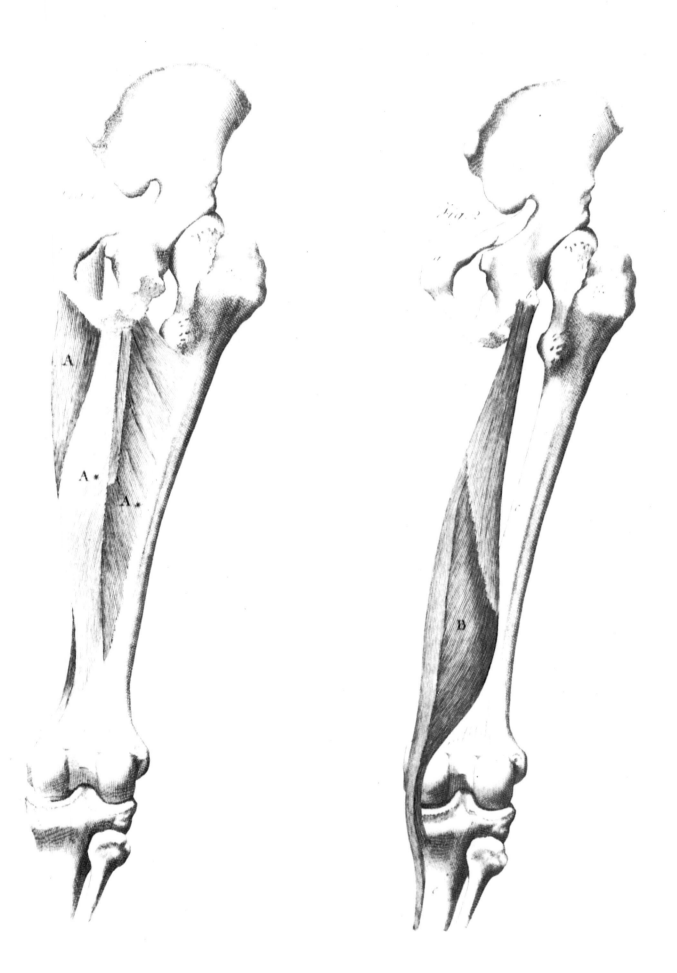

PLATE 79
GIUSEPPE DEL MEDICO, *Anatomia per Uso dei Pittori e Scultori*, 1811, Tavola 29. The
muscles of the upper leg.

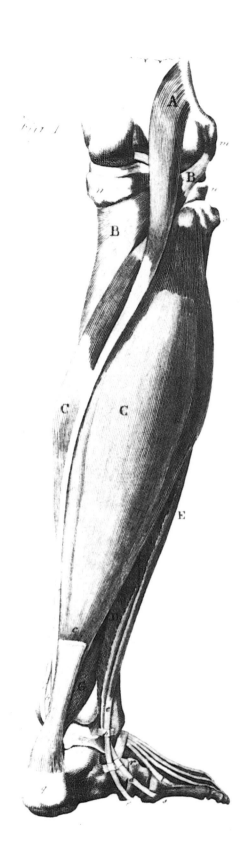

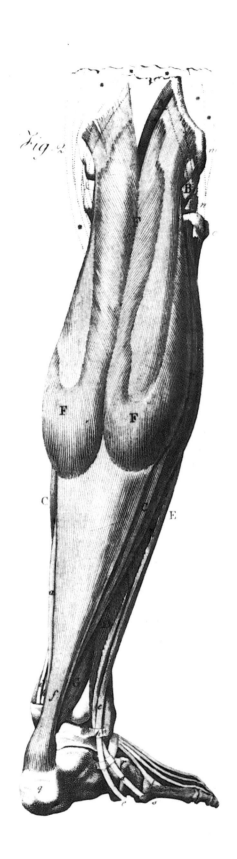

PLATE 80
GIUSEPPE DEL MEDICO, *Anatomia per Uso dei Pittori e Scultori*, 1811, Tavola 31. The
muscles of the lower leg, seen from the back.

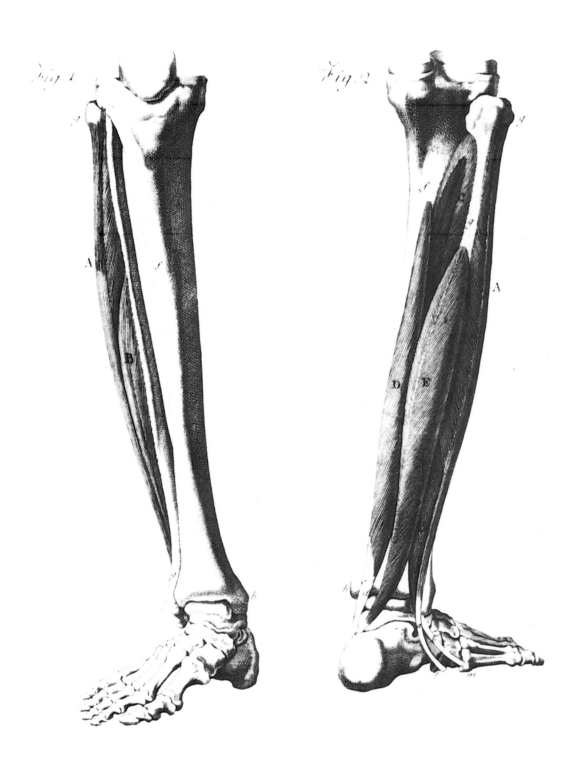

PLATE 81

GIUSEPPE DEL MEDICO, *Anatomia per Uso dei Pittori e Scultori*, 1811, Tavola 32. The bones
and muscles of the lower leg and foot.

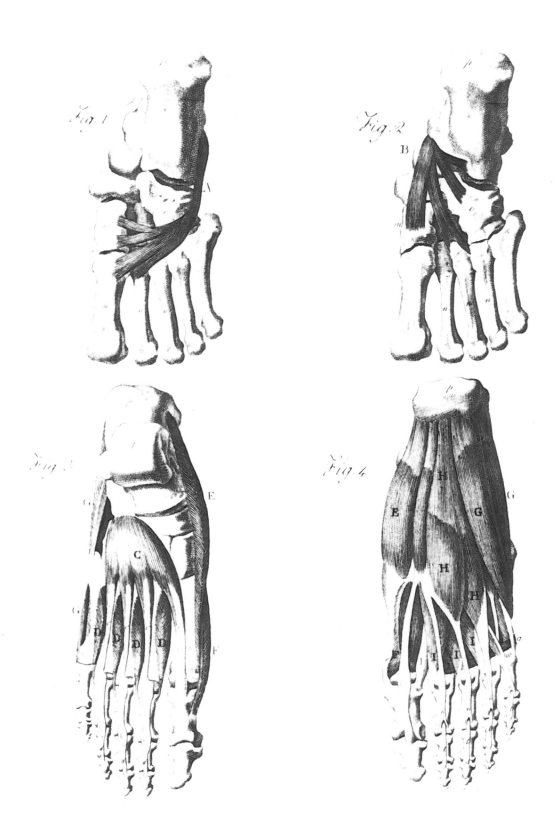

PLATE 82
Giuseppe del Medico, *Anatomia per Uso dei Pittori e Scultori*, 1811, Tavola 33. The bones
and muscles of the foot.

PLATE 83

Giuseppe del Medico, *Anatomia per Uso dei Pittori e Scultori*, 1811, Tavola 34. Like Cheselden (see plate 25), del Medico makes use of classical statue to illustrate his point, presumably because this represented the 'ideal' human form. Del Medico uses the famous Borghese gladiator here seen from the front.

PLATE 84

Giuseppe del Medico, *Anatomia per Uso dei Pittori e Scultori*, 1811, Tavola 35. The back
view of the statue seen in Plate 83.

TRAITÉ D'ANATOMIE TOPOGRAPHIQUE, OU ANATOMIE DES RÉGIONS DU CORPS HUMAIN
(1826)

by

Philippe – Frédéric Blandin

Artist: Nicolas Henri Jacob

Lithographed by Langlume

Photographs: Bernard Quaritch

Blandin was a surgeon at the Hôtel Dieu and Professor of Surgery at the Medical Faculty of Paris. He developed a number of new surgical techniques and in this book sought to integrate and demonstrate the relationship between anatomy and surgery. The book is aimed at those wishing to carry out operations.

Jacob's drawings were lithographed by Langlume, producing an image far closer to the original than could have been achieved through engraving.

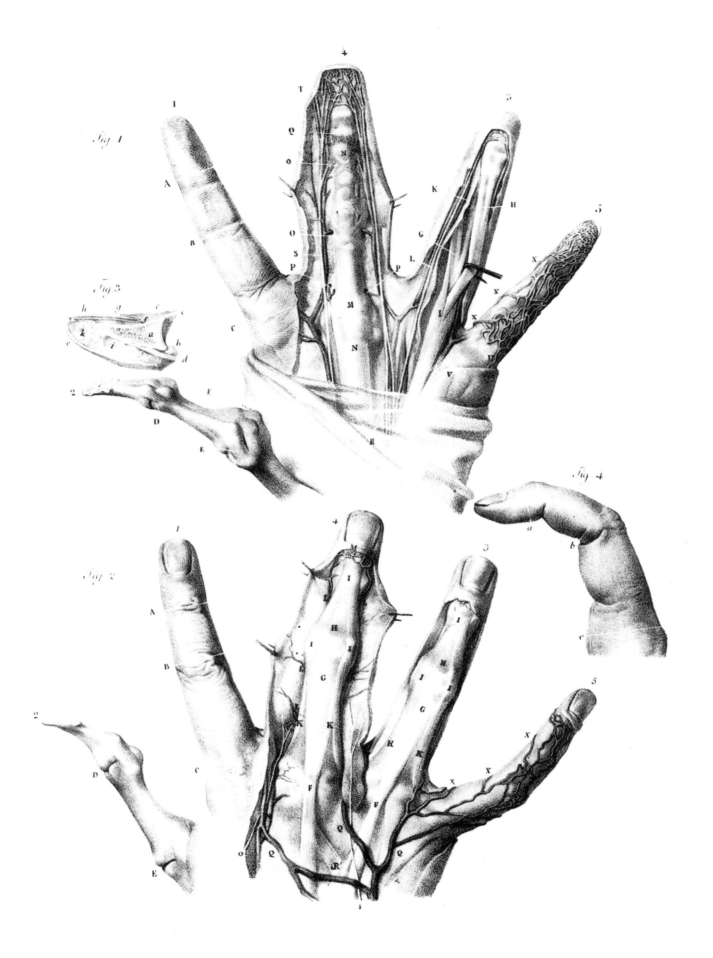

PLATE 85

Philippe-Frédéric Blandin, *Traité d'Anatomie Topographique ou Anatomie des Régions du Corps Humain*, 1826, Plate 1. Drawn by Nicholas Henri Jacob and lithographed by Langlume. The hand and fingers, seen from the front and back, with details including a longitudinal cut through the last section of a finger, bent and seen from the side to show the articulation.

PLATE 86

PHILIPPE-FRÉDÉRIC BLANDIN, *Traité d'Anatomie*, 1826, Plate 4. Drawn by Jacob and
lithographed by Langlume. The muscles of the neck. Compare the immense detail of this
illustration to Gray's much more diagramatic approach (see plate 114).

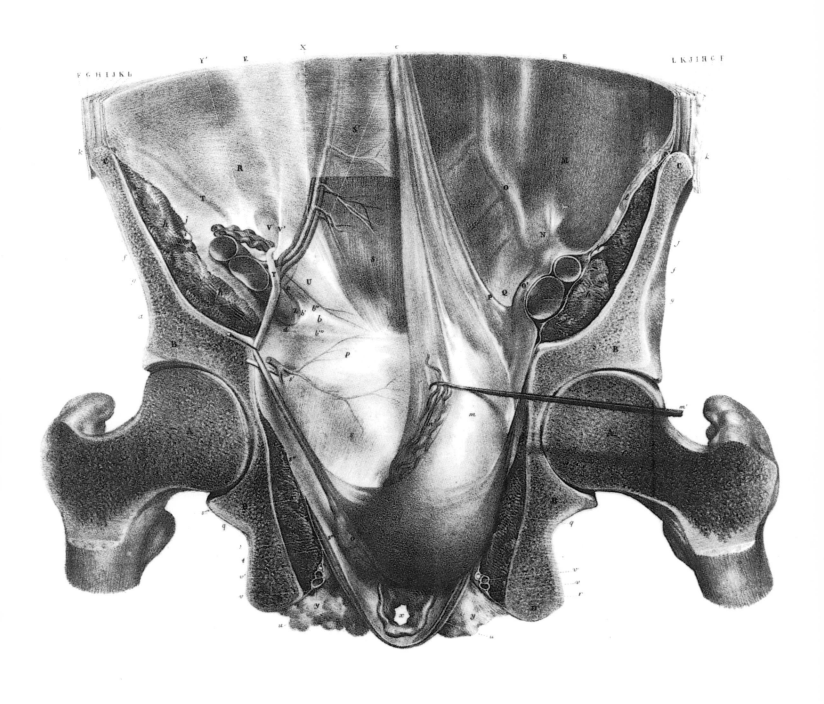

PLATE 87
PHILIPPE-FRÉDÉRIC BLANDIN, *Traité d'Anatomie*, 1826, Plate 7. Drawn by Jacob and
lithographed by Langlume. View of the lower abdomen.

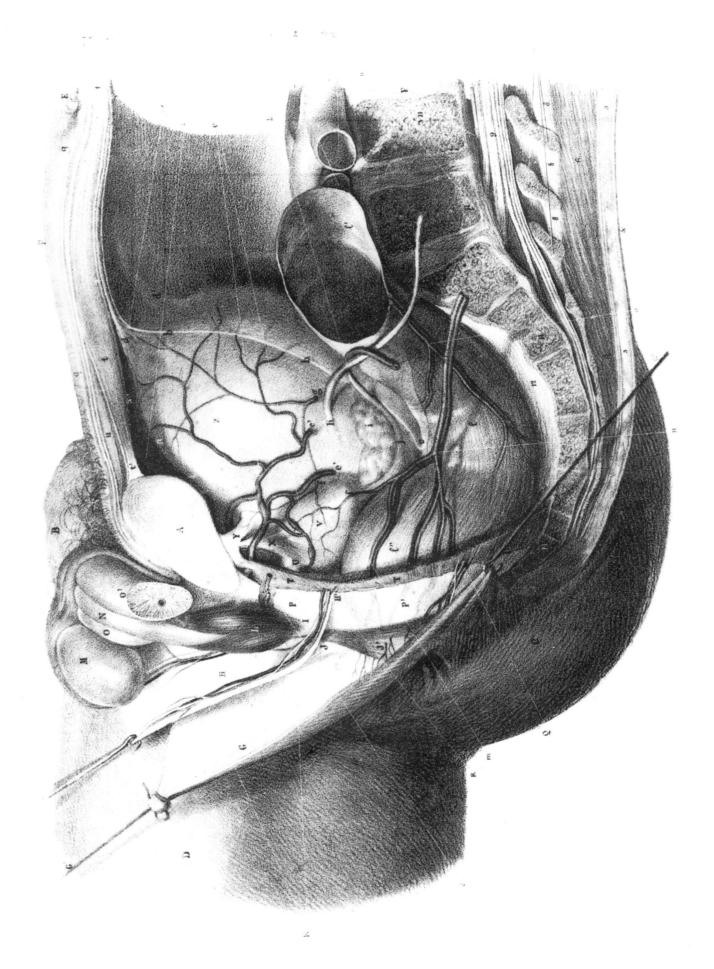

PLATE 88

Philippe-Frédéric Blandin, *Traité d'Anatomie*, 1826, Plate 10. Drawn by Jacob and
lithographed by Langlume. Side view of the lower abdomen.

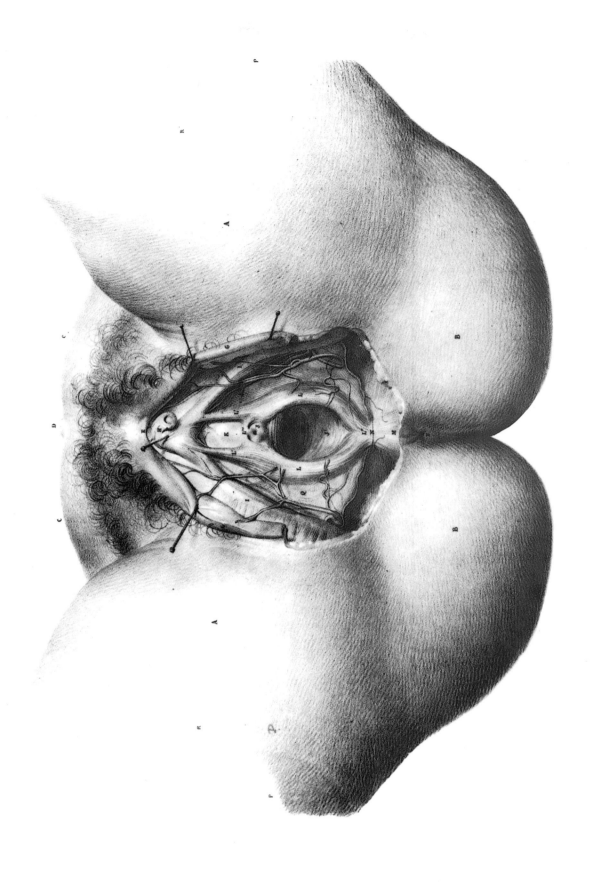

PLATE 89

Philippe-Frédéric Blandin, *Traité d'Anatomie*, 1826, Plate 11. Drawn by Jacob and lithographed by Langlume. Female genito-urinary area.

ANATOMICAL STUDIES OF THE BONES AND MUSCLES FOR THE USE OF ARTISTS (1833)

by

John Flaxman R.A.

Engraved by Henry Landseer

Photographs: Studio Editions

Flaxman's original chalk drawings were faithfully copied by Henry Landseer, who engraved them, using mezzotint for the shaded areas. Flaxman was more concerned with pose than with details: although his figures were drawn from life, they reflect his own neo-classical style in sculpture more than they do a precise, scientific reality.

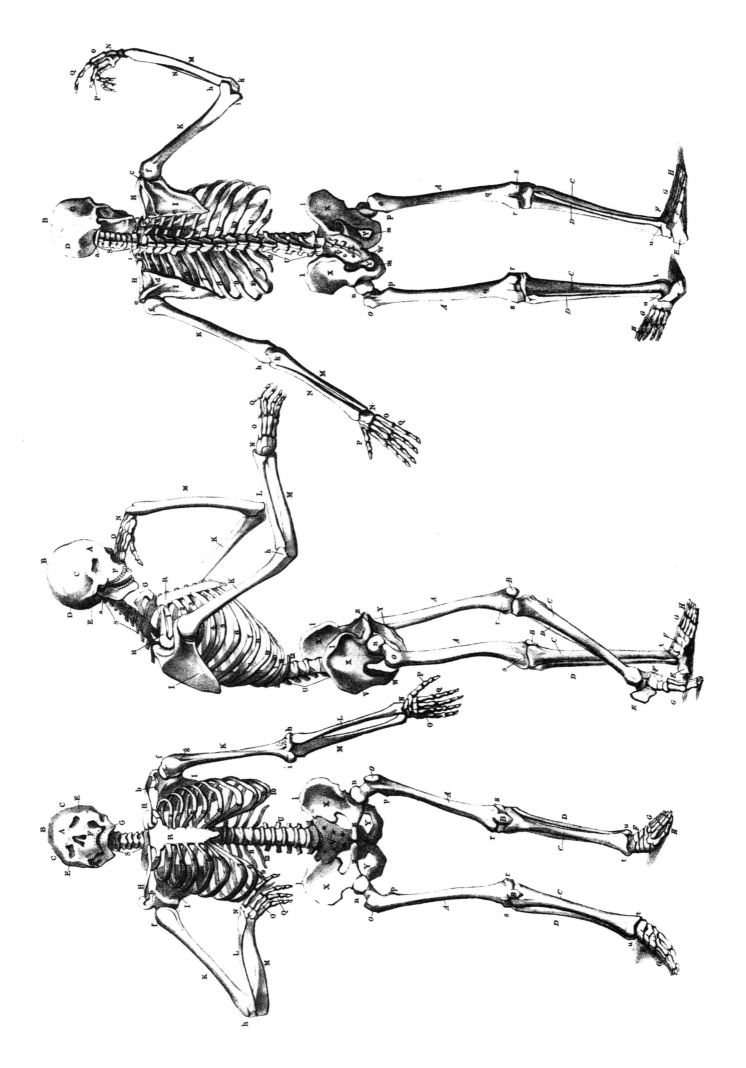

PLATE 90
JOHN FLAXMAN, *Anatomical Studies of the Bones and Muscles for the Use of Artists*, 1833,
Plate I. Drawn by John Flaxman and engraved by Henry Landseer. The stance of Flaxman's
skeletons is unusual and humorous.

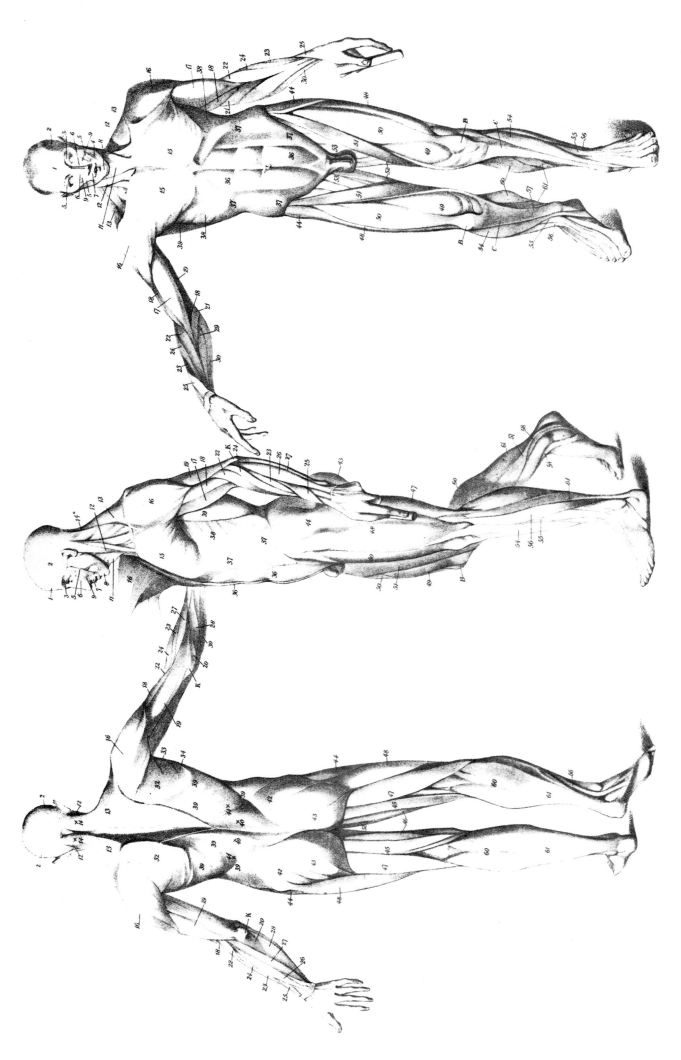

PLATE 91

JOHN FLAXMAN, *Anatomical Studies*, 1833, Plate 2. Drawn by John Flaxman and engraved
by Henry Landseer. These figures showing the muscles of the front, back and side are drawn
in a style which reflects Flaxman's preoccupation with sculpture.

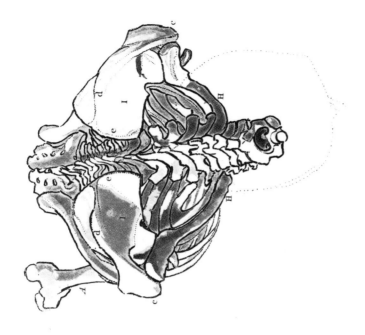

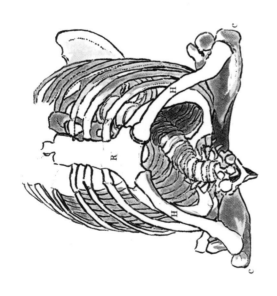

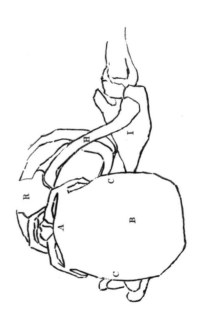

PLATE 92

JOHN FLAXMAN, *Anatomical Studies*, 1833, Plate 3. Drawn by John Flaxman and engraved
by Henry Landseer. These foreshortened views of the rib cage would have been of
considerable use to artists but are not intended to give precise information about skeletal
structure.

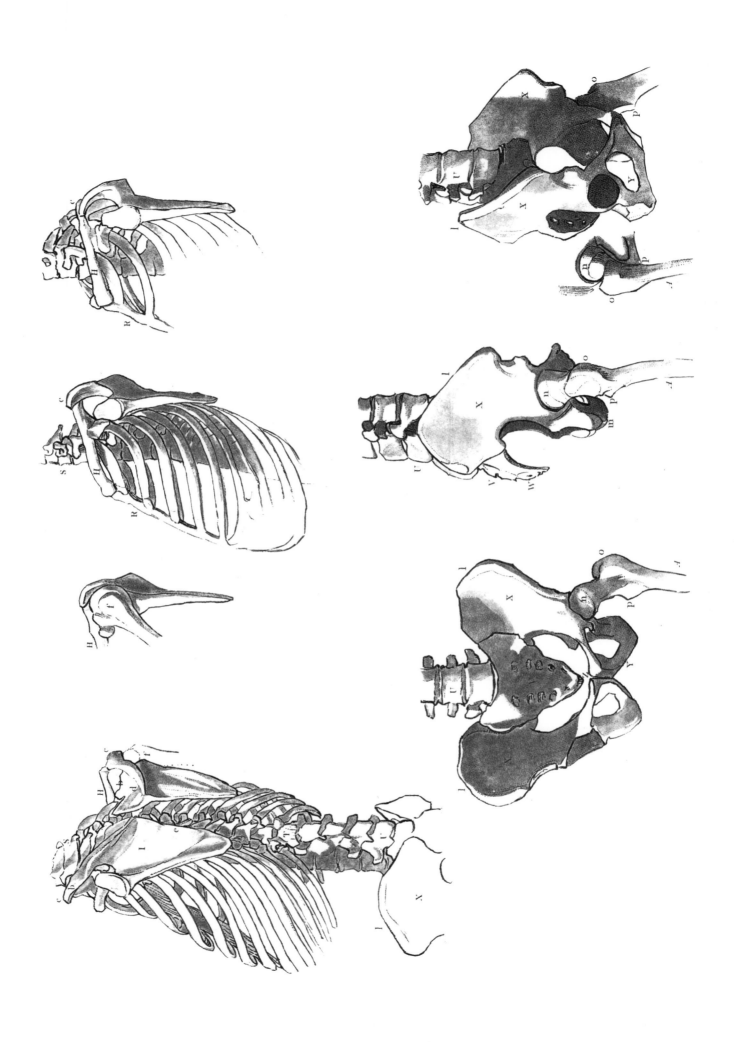

PLATE 93
JOHN FLAXMAN, *Anatomical Studies*, 1833, Plate 4. Drawn by John Flaxman and engraved
by Henry Landseer. Studies of the rib cage and pelvis.

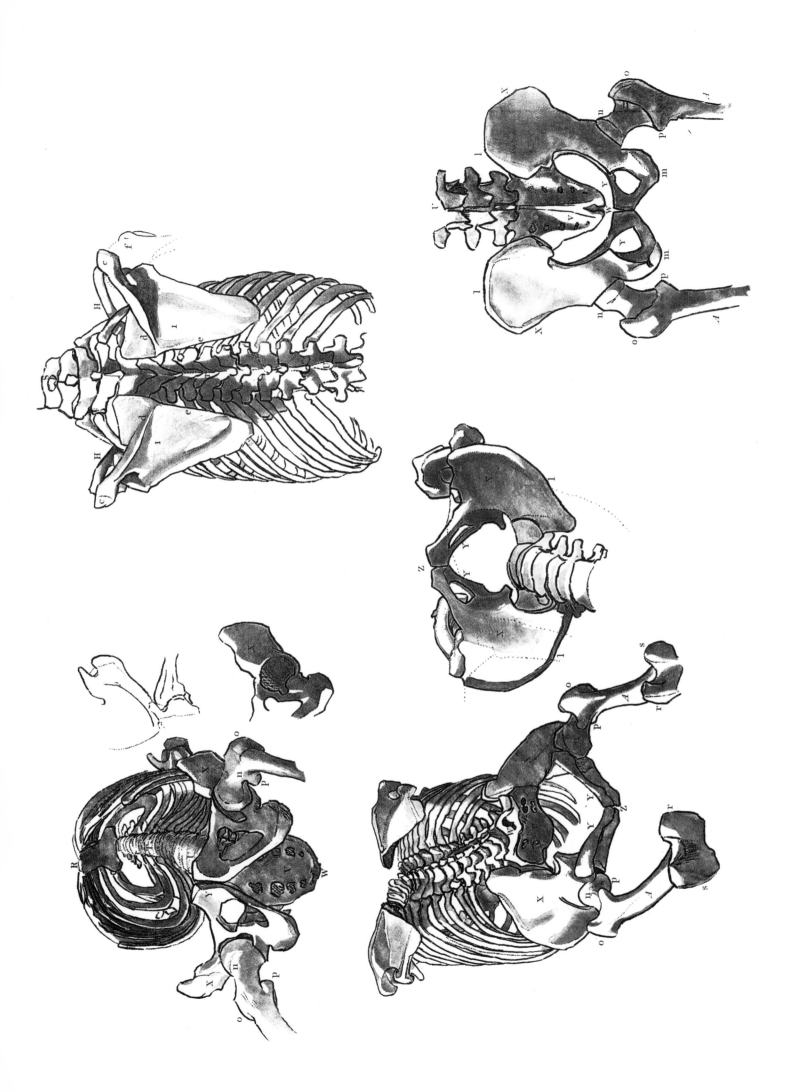

PLATE 94

JOHN FLAXMAN, *Anatomical Studies*, 1833, Plate 5. Drawn by John Flaxman and engraved
by Henry Landseer. Studies of the rib cage and pelvis.

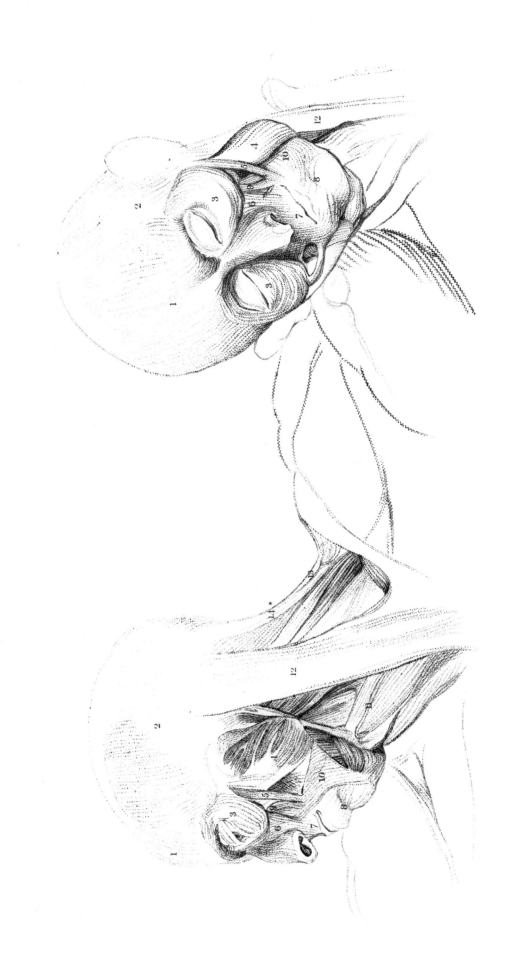

PLATE 95

JOHN FLAXMAN, *Anatomical Studies*, 1833, Plate 6. Drawn by John Flaxman and engraved
by Henry Landseer. The muscles of the head and neck.

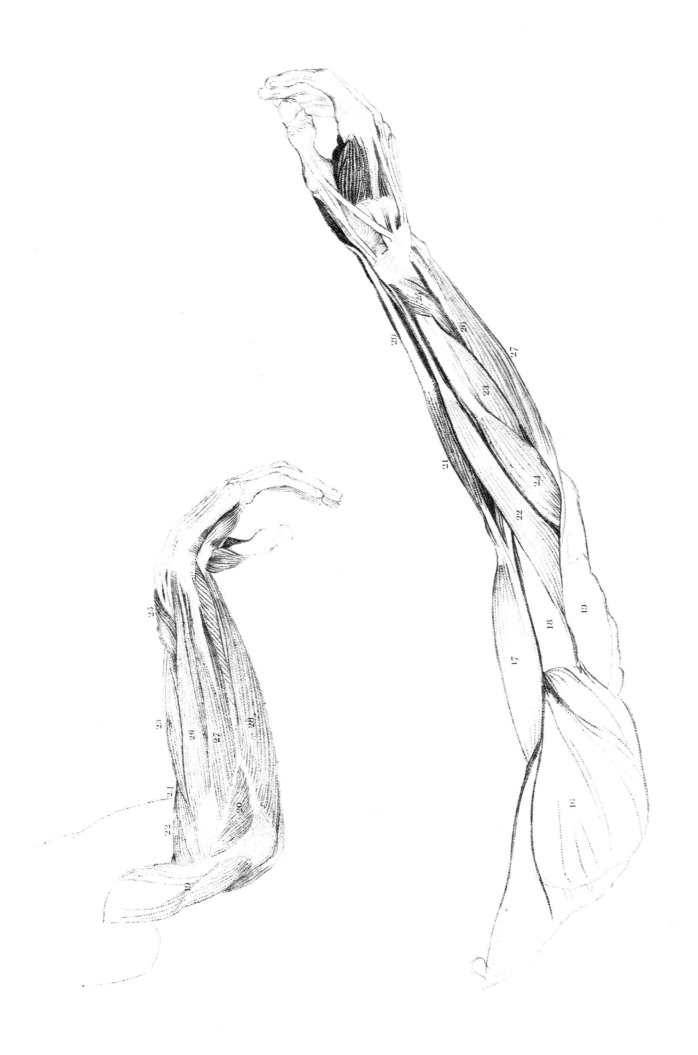

PLATE 96

JOHN FLAXMAN, *Anatomical Studies*, 1833, Plate 7. Drawn by John Flaxman and engraved
by Henry Landseer. The muscles of the arm and hand.

PLATE 97

JOHN FLAXMAN, *Anatomical Studies*, 1833, Plate 8. Drawn by John Flaxman and engraved
by Henry Landseer. The muscles of the arm and hand with the arm bent at the elbow and seen
from the front and the back.

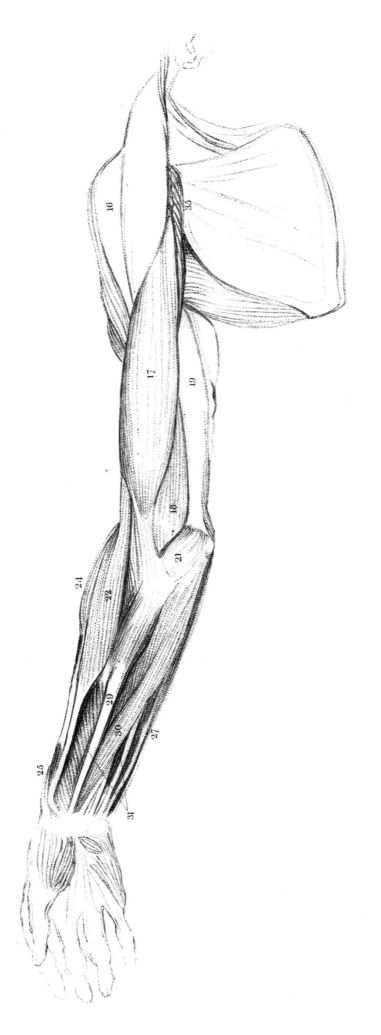

PLATE 98

JOHN FLAXMAN, *Anatomical Studies*, 1833, Plate 9. Drawn by John Flaxman and engraved by Henry Landseer. The muscles of the arm.

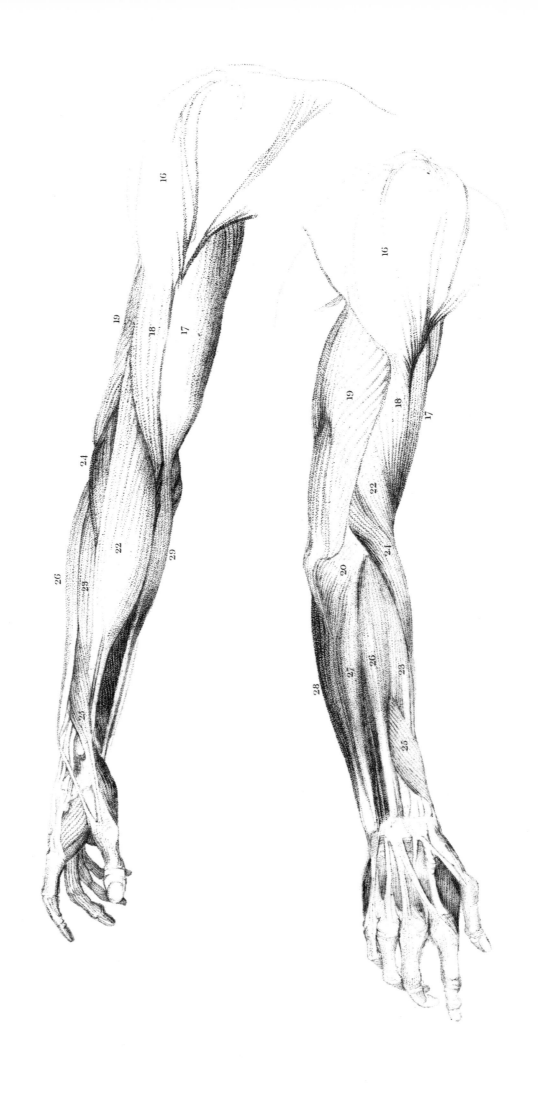

PLATE 99
JOHN FLAXMAN, *Anatomical Studies*, 1833, Plate 10. Drawn by John Flaxman and engraved
by Henry Landseer. The muscles of the arm.

PLATE 100
JOHN FLAXMAN, *Anatomical Studies*, 1833, Plate 11. Drawn by John Flaxman and engraved
by Henry Landseer. The muscles of the arm and torso.

PLATE 101

JOHN FLAXMAN, *Anatomical Studies*, 1833, Plate 12. Drawn by John Flaxman and engraved
by Henry Landseer. The muscles of the arm, neck and torso.

PLATE 102

Jᴏʜɴ Fʟᴀxᴍᴀɴ, *Anatomical Studies*, 1833, Plate 13. Drawn by John Flaxman and engraved
by Henry Landseer. The muscles of the arm, neck and torso.

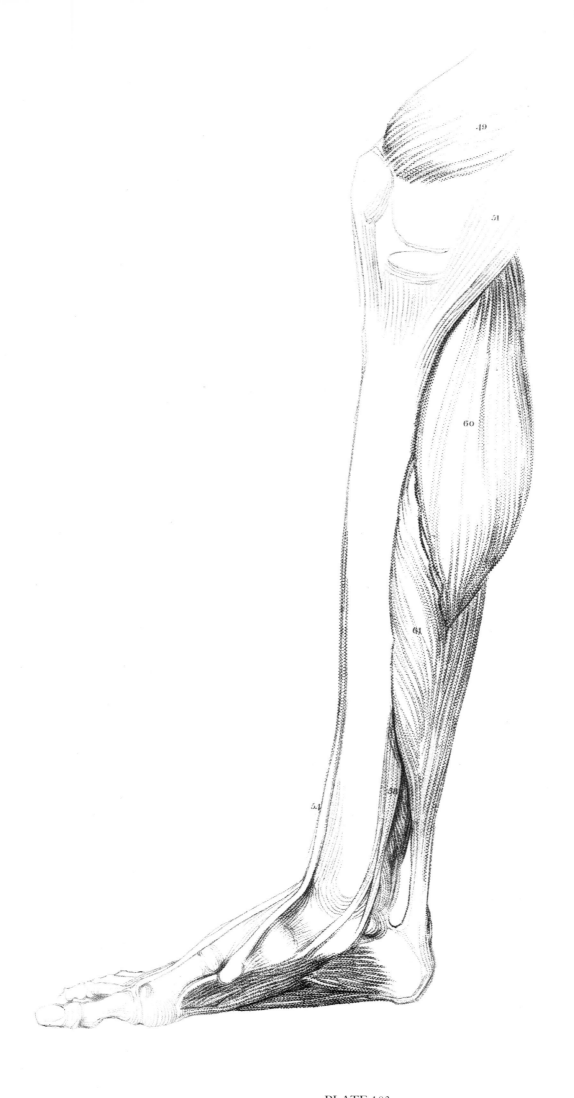

PLATE 103

JOHN FLAXMAN, *Anatomical Studies*, 1833, Plate 14. Drawn by John Flaxman and engraved
by Henry Landseer. The muscles of the inner side of the lower leg.

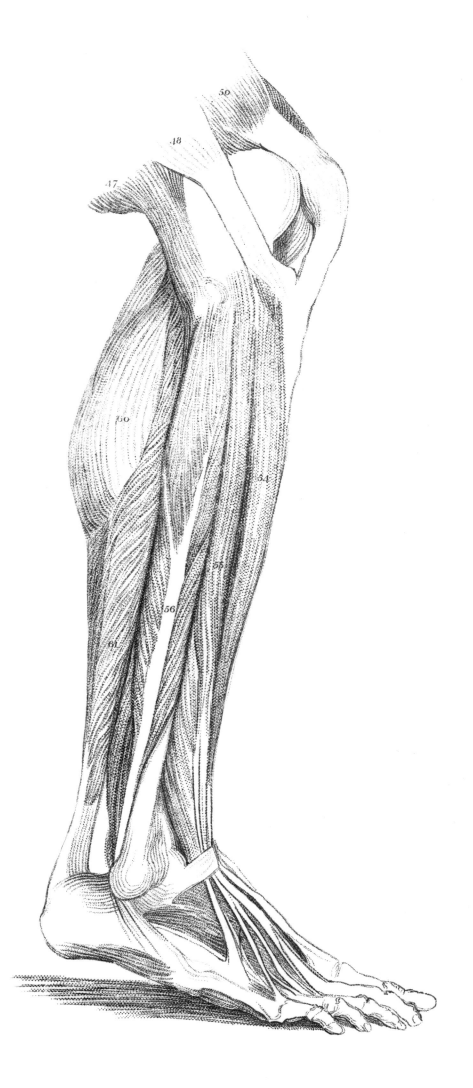

PLATE 104
JOHN FLAXMAN, *Anatomical Studies*, 1833, Plate 15. Drawn by John Flaxman and engraved
by Henry Landseer. The muscles of the outer side of the lower leg.

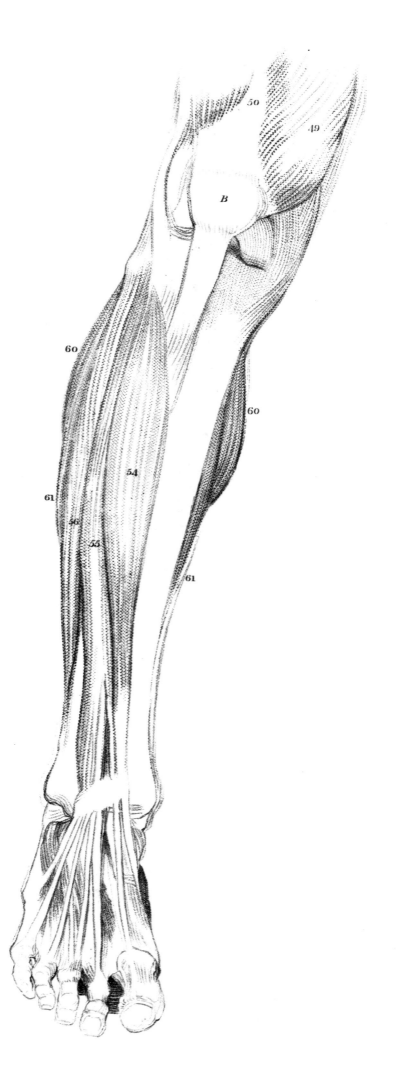

PLATE 105

JOHN FLAXMAN, *Anatomical Studies*, 1833, Plate 16. Drawn by John Flaxman and engraved
by Henry Landseer. The muscles of the front of the lower leg.

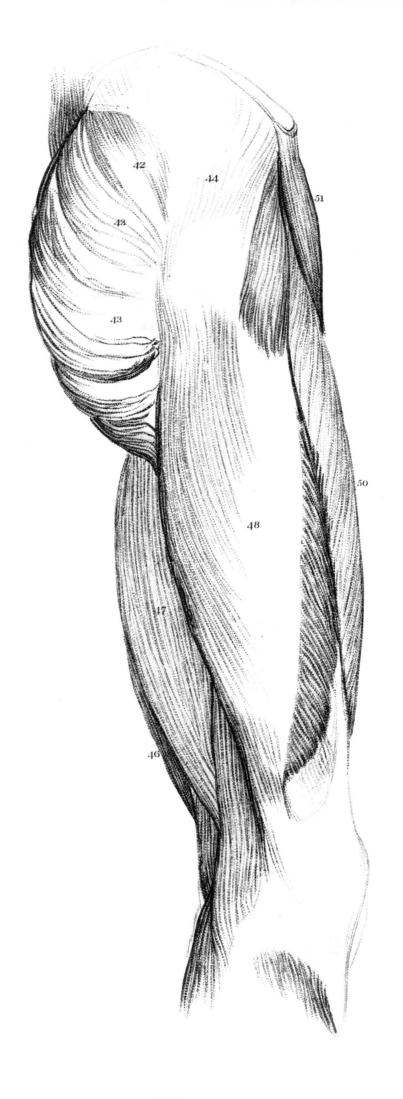

PLATE 106

JOHN FLAXMAN, *Anatomical Studies*, 1833, Plate 17. Drawn by John Flaxman and engraved
by Henry Landseer. The muscles of the outer side of the upper part of the leg.

PLATE 107
JOHN FLAXMAN, *Anatomical Studies*, 1833, Plate 18. Drawn by John Flaxman and engraved
by Henry Landseer. The muscles of the front and back of the upper part of the leg.

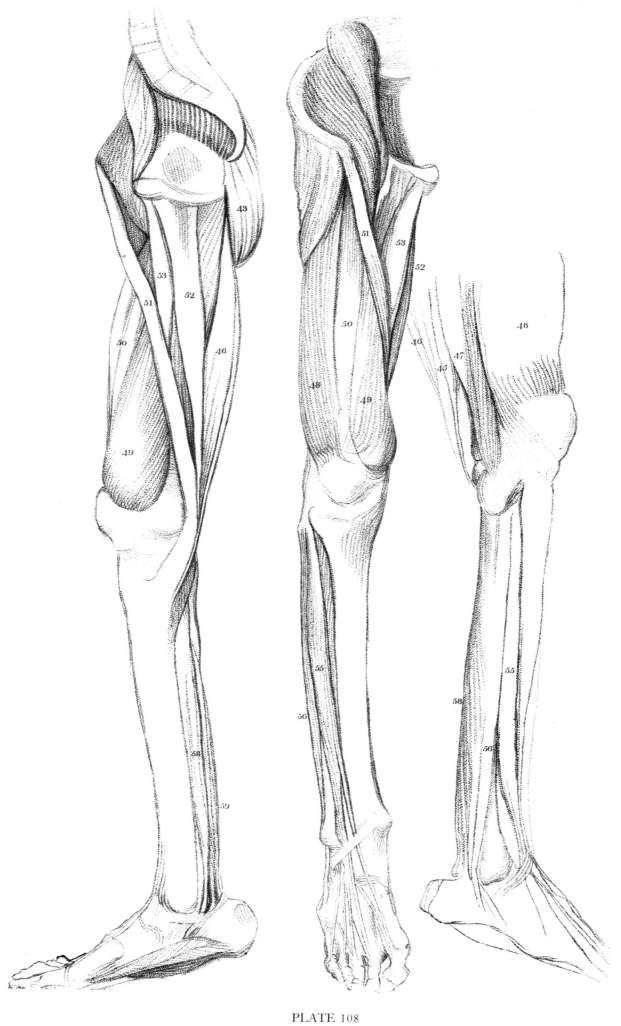

PLATE 108

JOHN FLAXMAN, *Anatomical Studies*, 1833, Plate 19. Drawn by John Flaxman and engraved by Henry Landseer. This illustration, and Plate 109, show the muscles of the leg but this time stripped down much further than the previous studies which are really concerned with surface anatomy.

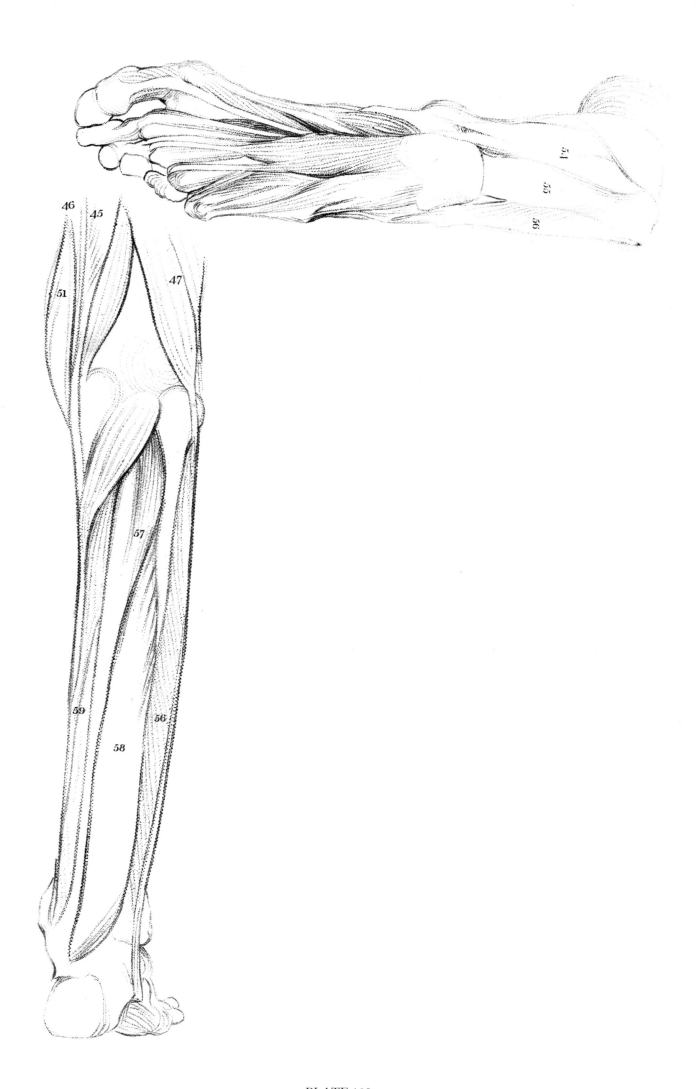

PLATE 109
JOHN FLAXMAN, *Anatomical Studies*, 1833, Plate 20. Drawn by John Flaxman and engraved
by Henry Landseer. The muscles of the leg and foot.

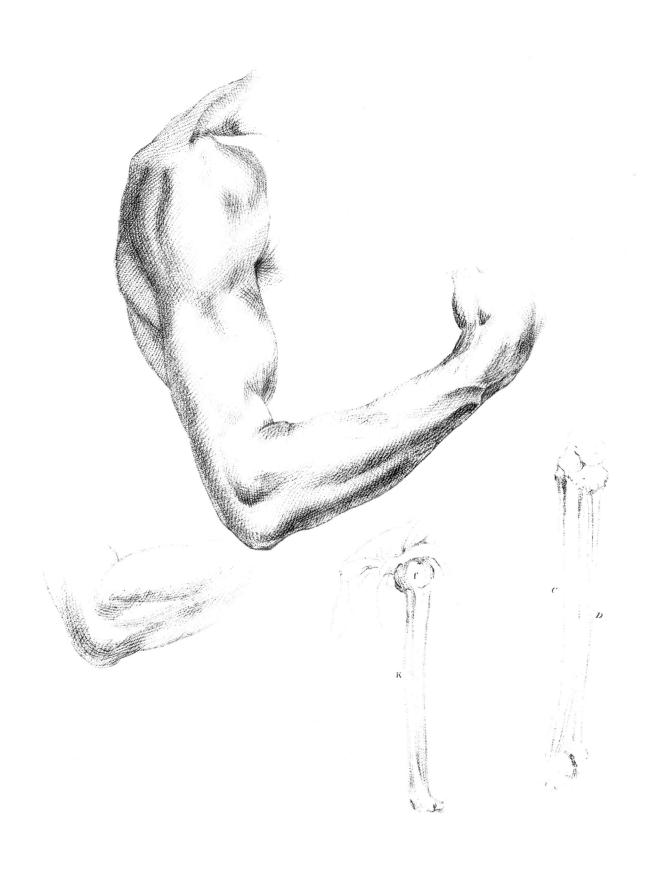

PLATE 110

JOHN FLAXMAN, *Anatomical Studies*, 1833, Plate 21. Drawn by John Flaxman and engraved
by Henry Landseer. This is strictly a figure drawing rather than an anatomical drawing since
it concerns itself purely with the surface, rather than what is beneath it. There are also two
sketches on the sheet of the bones of the upper arm.

ANATOMY (1858)

by

Henry Gray

Artist: H. Vandyke Carter

Photographs: British Museum

This illustrated treatise on general anatomy was the standard text book for English and American medical students. It appeared in many editions, reaching its fiftieth by 1918.

Gray's *Anatomy* is a good example of modern anatomical illustration: Carter's precise drawings serve the text, are diagrammatic and clearly labelled, and although the illustrations have considerable artistic merit, their purpose is no longer to be decorative.

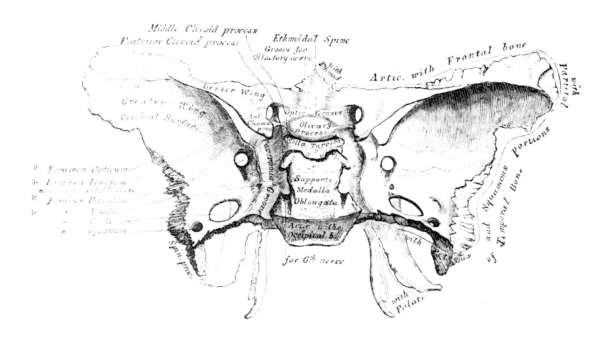

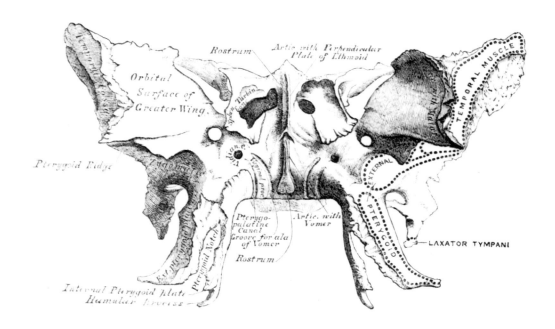

PLATE 111

Henry Gray, *Anatomy*, 1858, Fig. 29. Drawn by H.V. Carter. The sphenoid bone,
superior surface above and anterior surface below.

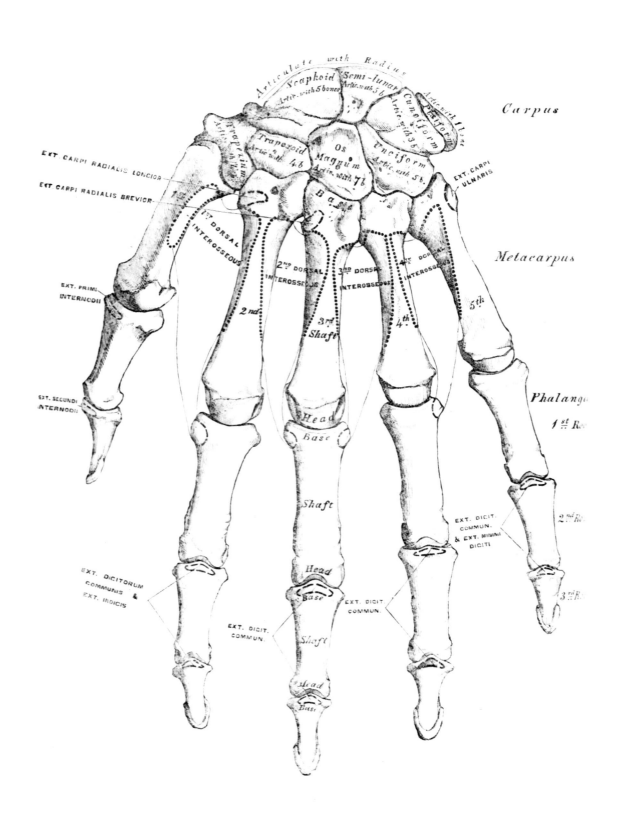

PLATE 112

Henry Gray, *Anatomy*, 1858, Fig. 84. Drawn by H.V. Carter. The bones of the left hand.

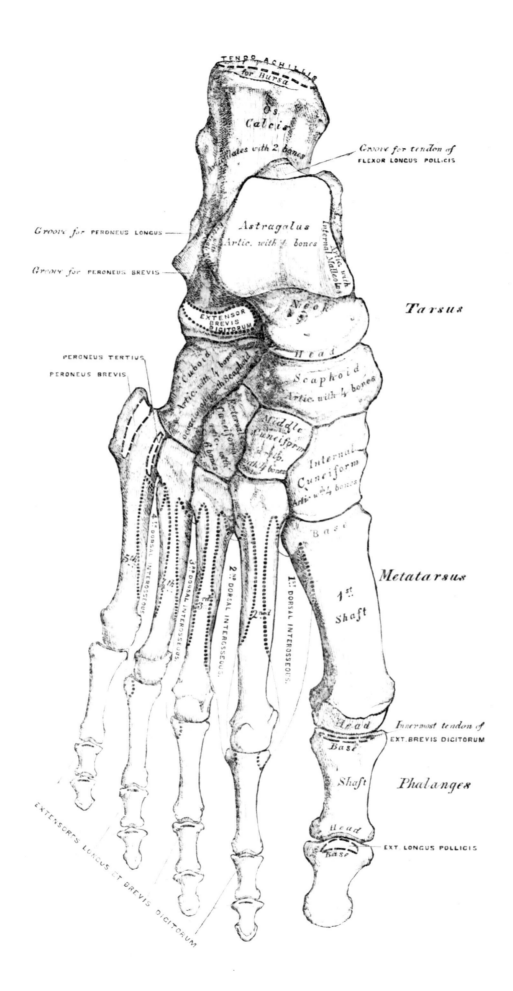

PLATE 113

HENRY GRAY, *Anatomy*, 1858, Fig. 96. Drawn by H.V. Carter. The bones of the right foot.

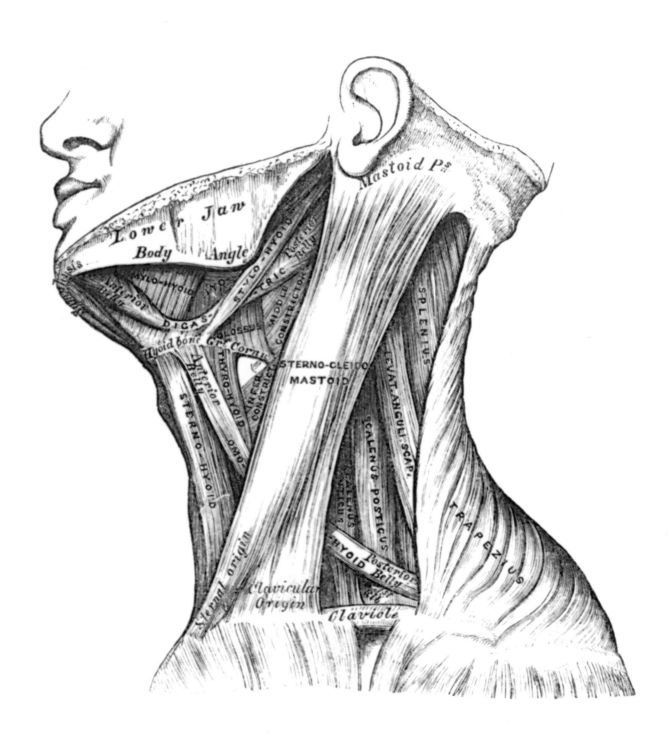

PLATE 114
Henry Gray, *Anatomy*, 1858, Fig. 136. Drawn by H.V. Carter. The muscles of the neck.

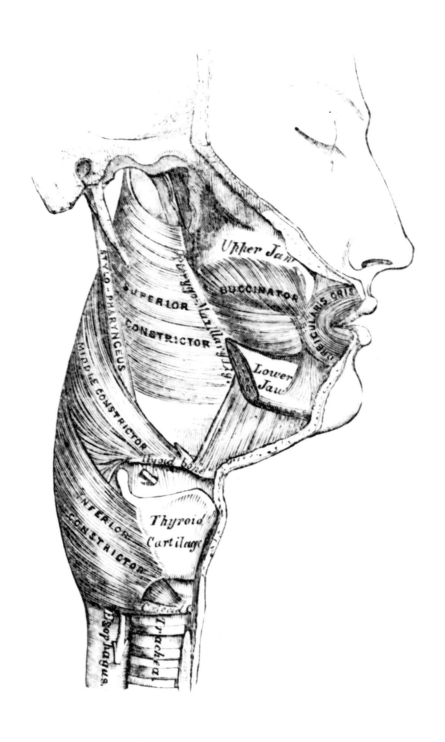

PLATE 115

HENRY GRAY, *Anatomy*, 1858, Fig. 139. Drawn by H.V. Carter. The muscles of the
pharynx, external view.

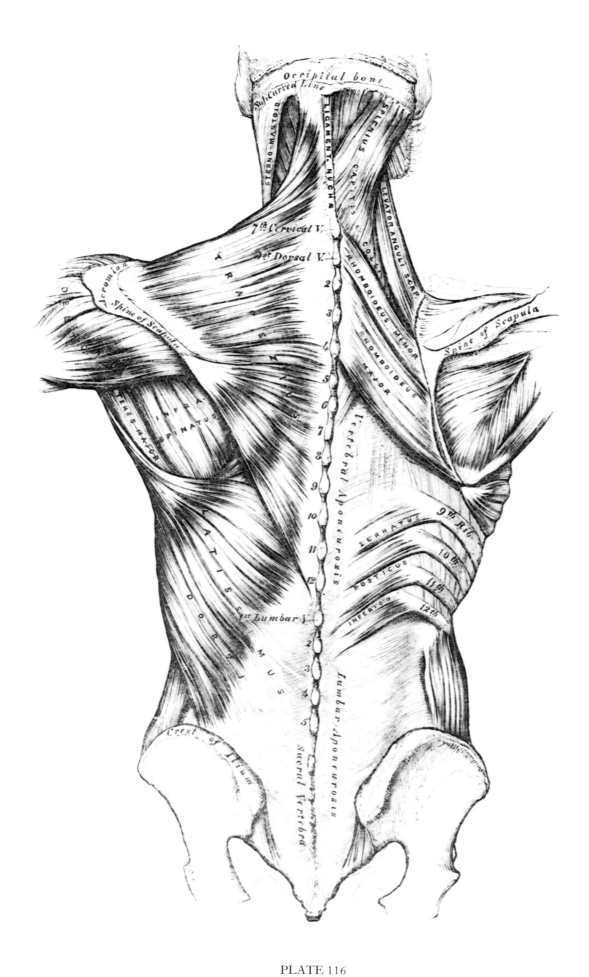

PLATE 116

HENRY GRAY, *Anatomy*, 1858, Fig. 143. Drawn by H.V. Carter. The muscles of the back.
'On the left side is exposed the first layer; on the right side, the second layer and part of the
third.'

PLATE 117
Henry Gray, *Anatomy*, 1858, Fig. 159. Drawn by H.V. Carter. The muscles of the left hand.

BIBLIOGRAPHY

ALBINUS, Bernhard, *Tabulae Sceleti*, 1747

BLANDIN, Ph.-Fred., *Traité d'Anatomie Topographique ou Anatomie des Régions du Corps Humain*, 1826

CAMPER, Petrus, *The Works of the Late Prof. Camper*, 1794

CHESELDEN, William, *Anatomy of the Humane Body*, 1712

CHESELDEN, William, *Osteographia*, 1733

EUSTACHIO, Bartolomeo, *Tabulae Anatomicae Clarissimi Viri*, ed. Lancisi, 1714

FLAXMAN, John, *Anatomical Studies of the Bones and Muscles for the use of Artists*, 1833

GRAY, Henry, *Anatomy*, 1858

HUNTER, John, *The Natural History of the Human Teeth*, 1771

HUNTER, William, *Gravid Uterus*, 1774

MEDICO, Giuseppe del, *Anatomia per uso dei Pittori e Scultori*, 1811

SANDIFORT, Eduard, *Museum Anatomicum Academiae Lugduno-Bataviae*, 1793–1835

SMELLIE, William, *Sett of Anatomical Tables*, 1754

VESALIUS, Andreas, *De Humani Corporis Fabrica*, 1543

FURTHER READING

BINDMAN, David, *John Flaxman RA*, catalogue to Royal Academy Exhibition, London, 1979

CHOULANT, Ludwig, *History and Bibliography of Anatomical Illustration*, English edition by Hafner Publishing Co., New York and London, 1962

DUNLOP, James M., *Anatomical Diagrams for the Use of Art Students*, G. Bell & Sons Ltd, London, 1899

HERRLINGER, Robert, *History of Medical Illustration*, Pitman Medical and Scientific Publishing Co Ltd., London, 1970

IRWIN, David, *John Flaxman 1755–1826 Sculptor, Illustrator and Designer*, Studio Vista/ Christies, published by Cassell Ltd., London, 1979

THORNTON, John L., *Jan van Rymsdyk*, Oleander Press, London, 1981